PAGE STREET
PUBLISHING CO.

To all of my Peanut Butter and Jilly readers, this book is for you! Without your support, it wouldn't be possible. I am thankful to every single one of you and hope this book inspires you to bake beautiful memories with the ones you love.

To my family and friends for your constant encouragement, recipe testing and never-failing love. You guys are the inspiration behind every sweet and savory recipe I create and I wouldn't be able to do it without you.

To God, for the great journey of life.

CONTENTS

INTRODUCTION

When I was a kid, I could eat anything I wanted without gaining a pound. But as my age increased, so did the number on the scale. I wanted to shed a few pounds, but I also knew that I was not someone who would ever be able to stick to a "diet." Why? Well, I love cookies too much. I knew the only way I'd be able to stick to a healthier lifestyle was if I was able to eat the foods I love! I began focusing on enjoying healthier and higher-quality foods, portion control, removing animal by-products and making each calorie count. I began cooking and baking lighter, vegan, often gluten-free, more nutritious versions of my favorite treats and comfort foods. I used simple, affordable ingredients found anywhere, and tried to keep my recipes quick, easy and full of flavor.

I found that looking forward to a sweet or savory treat each day kept me motivated and on track with my healthier lifestyle. I quickly saw results—dropping those extra pounds, and more importantly, feeling like my best self. Along with exercise, choosing whole foods, getting plenty of rest (when I'm not writing a book), hydration and a focus on balance, I have been able to maintain a weight I'm happy with by counting calories. That's why I include calories per serving for each of my recipes. Guys, part of self-love is feeding your body the nourishing foods you need and indulging in the sweet or savory treats you crave. It's why I eat healthy all day and never skip dessert—and you can, too!

Along my journey to better health and wellness, I learned more about the benefits of a plant-based diet. I had always struggled with inflammation, poor digestion and unbalanced energy. I noticed it seemed to get worse whenever I consumed meat or dairy. Removing those things made a world of a difference. It was life changing! As a certified carb lover, you can imagine my panic when I realized most of my favorite baked goods weren't vegan. Cakes, cookies, bread and biscuits . . . all of which are traditionally made with dairy and eggs. What was a new vegan with a passion for her oven to do? I looked online for recipes, finding most of them were complicated, high in calories and honestly, they didn't taste or look as good as the real thing. Rather than give up the goodies I loved, I decided to create my own vegan recipes for my favorite comfort foods. I started showing up to family events with my vegan baked treats in hand—within minutes, they would disappear. Everyone loved them and begged for the recipes, and many said they were "as good, if not better, than the real deal"! If I hadn't told them, they wouldn't have even known my recipes were vegan. That's how my blog, Peanut Butter and Jilly, was born.

I grew up baking with my mom on a regular basis. Whether made from scratch, boxed mixes or just picked up on an after-work/after-school grocery store run, baked goods were always around. For most of my childhood, it was just my mom and me. For us, baked goods were comfort; baking was therapy and it helped make our little apartment a home. Baking is about more than just enjoying something delicious, it's the satisfying process of measuring, mixing, stirring and—of course—taste testing. I love the process as much as I love the outcome. What tugs on my heartstrings the most, though, is helping others with dietary restrictions (like me) cook and bake delicious, better-for-you versions of family favorites. My first cookbook, *Easy Low-Cal Vegan Eats*, is dedicated to sharing my wholesome and nutritious vegan and gluten-free recipes for every meal of the day.

I put my whole heart into each breakfast, lunch, dinner, salad, soup and dessert recipe within that book. And I've poured my soul into each recipe found in this one!

I remember the first recipe I ever "low-cal veganized"—it was banana bread. I tested the recipe too many times to count until I landed on the perfect version. My Must-Try Banana Bread (page 80) is now one of my most popular recipes. It's made with oats and maple syrup, making it a better-for-you bread that is lower calorie, super-moist and almost too delicious for words. The batter is so good, you'll want to lick it from the bowl. And, since there are no raw eggs, you totally can!

Just like my famous banana bread, all the recipes in this book are easy, include straight-forward instructions and contain minimal ingredients. New to baking? No problem! My recipes are perfect for bakers of any skill level looking to watch their waistline without sacrificing flavor. Every single one is vegan, under 300 calories and dang delicious. Each can also be adapted to fit your gluten-free lifestyle, if needed—and perhaps best of all, most of them can be made in under 30 minutes.

This book is a collection of my favorite homemade bakes. These recipes hit close to home and even closer to the sweet spot. I've baked my memories right into each delicious vegan treat. Serving pumpkin pie (page 68) to Dad on Thanksgiving . . . fighting over the last donut (pages 117, 132 and 143) with my siblings . . . waking up to biscuits (pages 84, 96 and 144) for breakfast . . . celebrating life's big moments with cupcakes, cakes and loved ones. Let's face it: Baked goods make everyone smile. Which is why each scrumptious and mouthwatering recipe in this book is inspired by my most deliciously joyful moments . . . and I hope it inspires you to bake beautiful memories of your own.

VEGAN BAKING ESSENTIALS

As I mentioned earlier, my recipes are as easy to make as they are delicious! The ingredients you need are affordable and can be found almost anywhere.

Nondairy Milk: Unsweetened almond milk is my preference; however, any low-fat nondairy milk, such as oat, soy or low-fat coconut, usually works. Just be careful not to use full-fat canned coconut milk unless the recipe specifically lists it.

Nondairy Butter, Oils and Cream Cheese: Vegan butter is used throughout the book and is easily found near the regular butter at almost any grocery store. You may use any vegan butter in stick or tub form. My favorite brands include Miyoko's, Country Crock Plant Butter and Earth Balance. It's usually okay to substitute coconut oil (though it has a slightly sweeter taste). When using melted coconut oil, be careful not to mix it with cold liquid, or else it will solidify. Instead, use lukewarm or room-temperature liquids when mixing anything with melted coconut oil in your batters. Avocado oil and olive oil can also be used interchangeably in place of vegan butter in my recipes. Vegan cream cheese can be found near the regular cream cheese or in the produce department near the tofu at almost any grocery store. My favorite vegan cream cheese brands include Kite Hill and Miyoko's.

Flaxseed Meal: You will often see me use a mixture of flaxseed meal with warm water to create something we call "flax eggs," a vegan egg substitute that acts as a binder, bringing chewiness and moisture to baked goods. Just as important, flaxseed is also a great source of nutrients and fiber, making recipes more filling.

Sugar and Sweeteners: I use various sweeteners throughout this book. I commonly use pure maple syrup, organic cane sugar and pure powdered stevia because they are familiar and readily available. Every sweetener is different, though, and it's important to know how they vary so you can make sure you're using them correctly.

Coconut sugar, table sugar and cane sugar can usually be used interchangeably at the same measurements. Coconut sugar contains a fiber that helps keep your blood sugar levels from spiking. It has a maltier flavor than cane or table sugar.

Pure powdered stevia is a zero-calorie sweetener that can be used to reduce calories and sugar in a recipe. Keep in mind that it is much sweeter than sugar. For ½ cup (100 g) of sugar, use only 1 to 2 teaspoons (2 to 5 g) of stevia.

Monk fruit sweetener with erythritol (such as Lakanto brand) is another zero-calorie sugar substitute that I prefer. The taste is similar to brown sugar. It's about twice as sweet as regular sugar, so if the recipe calls for 1 cup (200 g) of sugar, I'll start with ½ cup (100 g) of monk fruit sweetener erythritol blend and adjust to taste.

Flour: I can't stress enough how important it is to use the proper flour in baking. The correct flour will work miracles. The wrong one can just make a mess. I usually use regular or gluten-free all-purpose flour as it is most widely and readily available. I also love working with all-purpose flour because most classic baked goods are made with it. So, the results are as close to the "real deal" as it gets.

When selecting gluten-free flours, read the labels carefully. My preferred product is King Arthur Gluten Free Measure for Measure Flour. It is almost identical to regular all-purpose flour. For best results, don't replace regular or gluten-free all-purpose flour with almond flour, coconut flour, baking flour or any other kind of flour. Another brand of gluten-free all-purpose flour I like is Cup4Cup.

Throughout this book, you will also see me use oats or oat flour, which are rich in minerals and vitamins. This is a nutritious alternative to regular all-purpose flour. Oats and oat flour contain more fiber, which helps keep you feeling fuller for longer. Another benefit of oats and oat flour is that they're naturally gluten-free. If you are gluten intolerant, check the labels to ensure that your oats and oat flour are certified gluten-free. While oats are naturally gluten-free, there could be cross-contamination with gluten-containing products during the company's manufacturing process. Only certified gluten-free products are guaranteed to not have had any contact with gluten-containing foods.

STORING BAKED GOODS

It's a good rule of thumb that most baked goods are best stored in an airtight container or wrapped in plastic on the countertop. Refrigerating baked goods can dry them out or make them dense. I like to wrap my breads and cakes in plastic wrap and then frost them before serving. I usually store my cookies in resealable plastic bags or a lidded storage container. The only baked goods I refrigerate in this book are the cinnamon rolls, baked oatmeals, cheesecakes, cobblers and pies because I find they last longer in the fridge. I usually reheat the oatmeal, cobblers and pies in the microwave before serving.

CRAVING COOKIES AND BROWNIES

Welcome to the first sweet spot of this book! As you know, I never skip dessert—and I've got a soft spot for homemade cookies, so it should come as no surprise that this chapter was the most fun to create (and taste test) and has a ton of love baked in.

Here, you'll find a few things that matter to me most about baking vegan cookies and brownies: Every recipe can be made gluten-free and in under 30 minutes. I'm one of those people who enjoys the taste of unbaked cookie dough and brownie batter almost as much as the baked goods themselves. And because there are no raw eggs used in any of the mixtures, feel free to nibble on the dough—guilt-free. You will want to devour these gooey brownies and chewy cookies. They are all addictive—don't say I didn't warn ya! But don't worry—they also clock in at under 300 calories, and in addition to being vegan, some include an even healthier twist.

Whether you're sinking your teeth into a batch of fudgy peanut butter swirled brownies (page 14), dunking the chocolaty Best Ever Brookie Cookies (page 13) into a glass of oat milk or diving into a plate of Jilly's Favorite Chewy Oatmeal Cookies (page 29), you're going to love every delectable bite.

Best Ever Brookie Cookies

The only way to improve upon a plate of chewy, buttery and sweet chocolate chip cookies that are baked to golden perfection: Add some brownie cookie dough! The result is a match made in chocolate lovers' heaven. These cookies are vegan, can be made gluten-free and everyone will love them. Dunk these into a glass of oat milk and you've got an unbelievably delicious dessert in just 15 minutes.

Are you in the mood for a batch of classic chocolate chip cookies or brownie cookies? Bake either of the cookie dough recipes on its own!

MAKES 36 cookies
ESTIMATED CALORIES:
105 per cookie

CHOCOLATE CHIP COOKIE DOUGH

2 tbsp (20 g) flaxseed meal

¼ cup (60 ml) warm water

½ cup (120 ml) melted vegan butter

1 cup (200 g) cane sugar (see Tip)

1 tsp vanilla extract

1 tsp baking powder

1 tsp unsweetened almond milk

¼ tsp salt

1¼ cups (156 g) regular or gluten-free all-purpose flour (for gluten-free, I like King Arthur Gluten Free Measure for Measure)

¼ cup (42 g) vegan chocolate chips

BROWNIE COOKIE DOUGH

2 tbsp (20 g) flaxseed meal

¼ cup (60 ml) warm water

½ cup (120 ml) melted vegan butter

1 cup (200 g) cane sugar (see Tip)

1 tsp vanilla extract

1 tsp baking powder

1 tsp unsweetened almond milk

¼ tsp salt

¼ cup (22 g) unsweetened cocoa powder

1 cup (125 g) regular or gluten-free all-purpose flour (for gluten-free, I like King Arthur Gluten Free Measure for Measure)

Preheat the oven to 425°F (220°C). Line a cookie sheet with parchment paper.

Prepare the chocolate chip cookie dough: In a small bowl, mix the flaxseed meal with the warm water. Set aside for 2 minutes, or until a gel forms, to make flax eggs.

In a medium-sized bowl, use a fork to mix together the flax eggs, melted vegan butter, sugar, vanilla, baking powder, almond milk and salt. Add the flour and mix until a thick cookie dough forms. Fold in the chocolate chips and set the dough aside.

Prepare the brownie cookie dough: In a small bowl, mix the flaxseed meal with the warm water. Set aside for 2 minutes, or until a gel forms, to make flax eggs. In a medium-sized bowl, use a fork to mix together the flax eggs, melted vegan butter, sugar, vanilla, baking powder, almond milk and salt. Add the cocoa powder and mix until smooth. Add the flour and mix until a thick cookie dough forms.

Scoop out about 1½ teaspoons (10 g) of each cookie dough and use your hands to roll the two different scoops of dough together into a ball. Place the ball on the prepared cookie sheet. Repeat until the pan is full, leaving about 2 inches (5 cm) between the dough balls.

Bake for 8 to 10 minutes, or until the cookies are golden around the edges and lift easily off the paper. Repeat until all the cookie dough has been baked. This recipe makes about 36 cookies.

TIP: Looking for a reduced-sugar option? Try using as little as ¾ cup (150 g) of sugar in place of the full cup (200 g) in each of the cookie doughs. Want to reduce the sugar even more? Try replacing the full cup (200 g) of sugar with ⅓ cup (66 g) of monk fruit sweetener with erythritol, resulting in a 65-calorie cookie!

Better-Than-The-Box Vegan Brownies with Peanut Butter Swirl

MAKES
12 brownies

ESTIMATED CALORIES:
241 per brownie with peanut butter / 176 per brownie without peanut butter

Are you one of those people who can't resist grabbing a box of brownie mix on their grocery run? Then you're going to love these super-chocolaty, perfectly moist vegan brownies. This recipe will have you kicking that boxed brownie mix to the curb because these are just as easy and way more delicious. Bake these as classic brownies or swirl in creamy peanut butter to take this batch of ooey-gooey goodness over the edge. I set out on a mission with one of my dearest friends to develop the perfect vegan brownie. Now, both she and her husband are hooked—and neither of them is vegan! Everyone who has tried this versatile recipe has told me the same thing: "They're better than the box!"

. . . .

Nonstick spray, for baking dish

½ cup (120 ml) melted vegan butter or coconut oil

⅓ cup (80 ml) unsweetened almond milk

1 cup (200 g) cane or coconut sugar (see Tip)

2 tsp (10 ml) vanilla extract

1 tsp baking powder

½ cup (44 g) unsweetened cocoa powder

1 cup (125 g) regular or gluten-free all-purpose flour (for gluten-free, I like King Arthur Gluten Free Measure for Measure)

¾ cup (126 g) vegan chocolate chips

½ cup (120 ml) melted creamy peanut butter (melt in a microwave)

Preheat the oven to 350°F (175°C). Spray an 8- to 9-inch (20- to 23-cm) baking dish with nonstick spray.

In a medium-sized bowl, use a fork to mix together the melted vegan butter, almond milk, sugar, vanilla, baking powder and cocoa powder until smooth. Mix in the flour until a brownie batter is formed. Spoon the batter into the prepared baking dish.

Fold in the chocolate chips, then spoon in the peanut butter and use your spoon to gently swirl the chocolate and peanut butter together, so the batter appears to be marbled. Or leave out the peanut butter to make classic brownies.

Bake for 30 minutes. The edges should be crisp, the top should be slightly cracked and the center will be gooey. Remove from the oven and allow to cool before cutting and enjoying the fudgy goodness.

TIP: Use ½ cup (100 g) of monk fruit sweetener with erythritol in place of the sugar for 186-calorie peanut butter–swirled brownies, or omit the peanut butter for 126-calorie fudgy brownies.

HEALTHY OAT FLOUR SWAP: Substitute the 1 cup (125 g) regular or gluten-free all-purpose flour with 1 cup plus 2 tablespoons (140 g) oat flour. This adds just 2 calories per brownie.

Apple Pie–Cinnamon Sugar Cookies

MAKES 20 cookies
ESTIMATED CALORIES:
120 per cookie
(without icing)

My first cookbook, *Easy Low-Cal Vegan Eats*, features an open-faced apple pie inspired by my pie-lovin' brother. Apple pie and sugar cookies are two of his (and most everyone's) favorite desserts. You really can't go wrong with either! These two classics are what inspired these delectably delicious cookies. They're vegan, you need only 20 minutes, and "oh, my apple pie," they are good!

. . . .

CINNAMON APPLES

1 tbsp (14 g) vegan butter, or nonstick spray, for saucepan

⅓ cup (42 g) peeled, cored and chopped Honeycrisp apple

½ tsp ground cinnamon

SUGAR COOKIE DOUGH

2 tbsp (20 g) flaxseed meal

¼ cup (60 ml) warm water

½ cup (120 ml) melted vegan butter

1 cup (200 g) cane sugar

1 tbsp (15 ml) unsweetened almond milk

1 tsp vanilla extract

1 tsp baking powder

¼ tsp salt

1¼ cups (156 g) regular or gluten-free all-purpose flour (for gluten-free, I like King Arthur Gluten Free Measure for Measure)

VANILLA ICING (ADDS 20 CALORIES PER COOKIE)

¾ cup (90 g) confectioners' sugar

1 tbsp (15 ml) unsweetened almond milk

1 tsp vanilla extract

Preheat the oven to 425°F (220°C). Line a baking sheet with parchment paper.

Prepare the cinnamon apples: Heat a small saucepan over medium heat with the vegan butter or nonstick spray. Once hot, add the apple and season with the cinnamon. Cook for 5 minutes, stirring frequently. Remove from the heat and set aside.

Prepare the sugar cookie dough: In a small bowl, mix the flaxseed meal with the warm water. Set aside for 2 minutes, or until a gel forms, to make flax eggs. In a medium-sized bowl, use a fork to mix together the melted vegan butter, cane sugar, flax eggs, almond milk, vanilla, baking powder and salt. Add the flour and mix until a cookie dough forms. Fold in the cinnamon apples.

Use your hands to roll about a tablespoon (20 g) of cookie dough into a ball. Place the ball on the prepared cookie sheet. Repeat until the baking sheet is full, spacing the balls about 1½ inches (4 cm) apart. You should have about 20 dough balls.

Bake for 9 to 11 minutes, or until the cookies are golden on the edges and they lift easily off the parchment paper.

While the cookies bake, prepare the vanilla icing: In a medium-sized bowl, combine the confectioners' sugar, almond milk and vanilla, and beat with a whisk or electric mixer until smooth.

Remove the cookies from the oven and allow them to cool before drizzling the icing over them and serving.

TIP: These cookies are 120 calories each without frosting. You can leave out the apples and icing and bake these as classic sugar cookies, if you prefer!

HEALTHY OAT FLOUR SWAP: Substitute the 1¼ cups (156 g) regular or gluten-free all-purpose flour with 2 cups (250 g) oat flour. This adds 16 calories per cookie.

Brown Sugar Chocolate Chip Cookies

There's just something about a freshly baked chocolate chip cookie—so buttery, soft, chewy and sweet. Typical recipes for them contain eggs, dairy and a bit too much sugar. And so many recipes ask you to refrigerate the dough. Does anyone else feel that waiting for cookie dough to chill in the fridge is the longest hour of your life? This recipe skips the eggs and dairy, uses just a little brown sugar—and needs no refrigeration: Simply mix, scoop, roll and bake! The result is a cookie so perfectly golden on the outside and soft on the inside that you're going to want to eat the entire batch! You won't feel too bad about it, as at only 92 calories a cookie, you can enjoy a few—guilt-free! PS: If you have any dough left over, nibble away. The perks of vegan baking!

MAKES 20 cookies

ESTIMATED CALORIES: 92 per cookie

· ·

2 tbsp (20 g) flaxseed meal

¼ cup (60 ml) warm water

½ cup (120 ml) melted vegan butter

¾ cup (165 g) light brown sugar, or cane or coconut sugar

1 tbsp (15 ml) unsweetened almond milk

1 tsp vanilla extract

½ tsp ground cinnamon (optional)

1 tsp baking powder

1¼ cups (156 g) regular or gluten-free all-purpose flour (for gluten-free, I like King Arthur Gluten Free Measure for Measure)

¼ cup (42 g) vegan chocolate chips

Preheat the oven to 425°F (220°C). Line a baking sheet with parchment paper.

In a small bowl, mix the flaxseed meal with the warm water. Set aside for 2 minutes, or until a gel forms, to make flax eggs.

In a medium-sized bowl, use a fork to mix together the flax eggs, melted vegan butter, brown sugar, almond milk, vanilla, cinnamon (if using) and baking powder. Then, mix in the flour until a thick cookie dough forms. Fold in the chocolate chips.

Use your hands to roll about a tablespoon (20 g) of cookie dough into a ball. Place the ball on the prepared cookie sheet. Repeat until the baking sheet is full, spacing the balls about 2 inches (5 cm) apart. You should have about 20 dough balls.

Bake for 8 to 10 minutes, or until the cookies are lightly golden around the edges and lift easily off the parchment paper. I love these served warm, dunked into oat milk.

HEALTHY OAT FLOUR SWAP: Substitute the 1¼ cups (156 g) regular or gluten-free all-purpose flour with 2 cups (250 g) oat flour. This adds 16 calories per cookie.

Better-for-You Peanut Butter Banana Blondies

MAKES
16 blondies

ESTIMATED CALORIES:
160 per blondie

One of my favorite flavor combinations is peanut butter and banana! If you're like me and crave peanut butter, you must try these delicious blondies. They're one of my all-time favorite treats because they're wholesome, filling and incredibly peanut buttery. They are waistline-friendly thanks to the filling oats and healthier sugar and flour options. If you wish, serve these blondies with a little peanut butter spread on top (life can always use more peanut butter), sliced banana or sprinkles.

Nonstick spray, for casserole dish

2 overripe bananas, mashed

½ cup (120 ml) unsweetened almond milk

½ cup (100 g) cane or coconut sugar (see Tip)

¼ cup (60 ml) melted coconut oil or vegan butter

½ cup (129 g) creamy peanut butter

1 tsp vanilla extract

1 tsp baking powder

1 cup (125 g) regular or gluten-free all-purpose flour (for gluten-free, I like King Arthur Gluten Free Measure for Measure)

2 cups (180 g) quick oats (certified gluten-free, if needed)

Preheat the oven to 375°F (190°C). Spray a 9 x 11–inch (23 x 28–cm) casserole dish with nonstick spray.

In a medium-sized bowl, use a fork or whisk to mix together the mashed bananas, almond milk, sugar, melted coconut oil, peanut butter, vanilla and baking powder until smooth. Add the flour and oats, and mix until a batter forms.

Pour the batter into the prepared casserole dish. Bake for about 20 minutes, or until lightly golden around the edges and completely risen in the center.

Remove from the oven and allow to cool completely before cutting into 16 squares and serving. These are absolutely delicious on their own, or spread with a bit of peanut butter on top and garnished with sprinkles for an even more delicious treat!

TIP: Want a sugar-free blondie? Swap out the sugar for monk fruit sweetener erythritol blend for 135 calorie blondies.

HEALTHY OAT FLOUR SWAP: Substitute the 1 cup (125 g) regular or gluten-free all-purpose flour with 1¼ cups (156 g) oat flour or 2 cups (250 g) almond flour. The oat flour swap adds 14 calories per serving and the almond flour swap adds 25 calories per serving.

Sweet Lemon Cookies

These are one of my newest cookie addictions! They're lemony and sweet served on their own, and taste even better when topped with almond milk glaze or tossed in confectioners' sugar. What could be better? These chewy cookies are perfectly golden on the outside with a light, crisp bite. Speaking of bite: You will have a hard time stopping at one, so these will go fast! Good thing these low-calorie treats take only about 20 minutes to bake.

MAKES 24 cookies
ESTIMATED CALORIES: 107 per cookie (without glaze)

LEMON COOKIES

2 tbsp (20 g) flaxseed meal

¼ cup (60 ml) warm water

1 cup (200 g) cane sugar (see Tip)

½ cup (120 ml) melted vegan butter or coconut oil

¼ cup (60 ml) fresh lemon juice

1 tsp vanilla extract

1 tsp baking powder

1 tbsp (15 ml) unsweetened almond milk

2 cups (250 g) regular or gluten-free all-purpose flour (for gluten-free, I like King Arthur Gluten Free Measure for Measure)

Confectioners' sugar, for dusting (optional)

VANILLA ALMOND MILK GLAZE (OPTIONAL; ADDS 24 CALORIES PER COOKIE)

1 cup (120 g) confectioners' sugar

2 tbsp (30 ml) unsweetened almond milk

1 tsp vanilla extract

Prepare the lemon cookies: Preheat the oven to 425°F (220°C) and line a baking sheet with parchment paper.

In a small bowl, mix the flaxseed meal with the warm water. Set aside for 2 minutes, or until a gel forms, to make flax eggs.

In a large bowl, use a fork to mix together the flax eggs, cane sugar, melted vegan butter, lemon juice, vanilla, baking powder and almond milk. Then, add the flour and mix until a thick cookie dough forms. The dough will be loose.

Use your hands to roll the dough into 24 balls and place them on your prepared baking sheet, spaced about 1½ inches (4 cm) apart.

Bake for 10 to 12 minutes, or until the cookies are golden on the bottom and lift easily off of the parchment paper.

Prepare the glaze (if using): In a small bowl, whisk together the confectioners' sugar, almond milk and vanilla. Allow the cookies to cool and then serve plain, brushed with the glaze or tossed in the confectioners' sugar (if using).

TIP: Want a lemony sweet cookie for under 100 calories a pop? Swap out the cane sugar for ½ cup (100 g) of monk fruit sweetener with erythritol, resulting in a 73-calorie cookie!

Nutter Butter Lover Cookies

MAKES 20 cookies
ESTIMATED CALORIES: 85 per cookie

Go Nutter Butter nuts over these chewy, buttery and ridiculously yummy peanut butter cookies. Thanks to the flaxseed meal, coconut oil, peanut butter powder and coconut sugar, they're a healthier alternative to conventional peanut butter cookies but every bit as dunkably delicious! My non-vegan, peanut butter–loving dad goes crazy over these. The plate gets cleared pretty quickly when I bake these for my family—and everyone is amazed when they find out they're vegan and take only 20 minutes to make!

2 tbsp (20 g) flaxseed meal

¼ cup (60 ml) warm water

½ cup (120 ml) melted vegan butter or coconut oil

¾ cup (150 g) coconut or cane sugar

1 tsp unsweetened almond milk

1 tsp vanilla extract

1 tsp baking powder

¼ tsp salt

¾ cup (72 g) powdered peanut butter

¾ cup (94 g) regular or gluten-free all-purpose flour (for gluten-free, I like King Arthur Gluten Free Measure for Measure)

Preheat the oven to 425°F (220°C). Line a baking sheet with parchment paper.

In a small bowl, mix the flaxseed meal with the warm water. Set aside for 2 minutes, or until a gel forms, to make flax eggs.

In a medium-sized bowl, use a fork to mix together the flax eggs, melted vegan butter, sugar, almond milk, vanilla, baking powder and salt. Mix in the peanut butter powder and flour until a thick cookie dough forms.

Using your hands, roll the dough into 20 balls and place them on the prepared baking sheet, leaving about 1½ inches (4 cm) of space between the balls.

Bake for 8 to 10 minutes, or until the cookies are golden around the edges and lift easily off the parchment paper. Serve warm with a side of oat milk and watch as they magically disappear off the plate.

HEALTHY OAT FLOUR SWAP: Substitute the ¾ cup (94 g) regular or gluten-free all-purpose flour with 1 cup (125 g) oat flour. This adds 6 calories per cookie.

Sugar Cookie Oatmeal Bake

SERVINGS: 8
ESTIMATED CALORIES:
216 per serving

Baked oatmeal is a staple in my home. And we all know I have a sweet spot for cookies. If your waistline is craving something a bit healthier than conventional cookies, you're going to love this tasty oatmeal bake. It's like a sugar cookie cake, but instead of flour, we use wholesome oats and healthy flaxseed meal. If you like the cookie cake on page 33, this is going to be a go-to for you! While baking, the oats take on all the buttery sugary flavors of a classic sugar cookie. The smell of this baking will draw everyone in and the result will be a golden and cozy sweet treat that everyone in your home will love.

Nonstick spray, for casserole dish

2 tbsp (20 g) flaxseed meal

¼ cup (60 ml) warm water

1 cup (240 ml) unsweetened almond milk

¼ cup (60 ml) melted vegan butter or coconut oil

¾ cup (150 g) cane or coconut sugar (see Tip)

1 tsp vanilla extract

1½ tsp (7 g) baking powder

2 cups (180 g) quick oats (certified gluten-free, if needed)

3 tbsp (36 g) rainbow sprinkles

Preheat the oven to 350°F (175°C). Spray a 9 x 11–inch (23 x 28–cm) casserole dish with nonstick spray.

In a small bowl, mix the flaxseed meal with the warm water. Set aside for 2 minutes, or until a gel forms, to make flax eggs.

In a large bowl, use a fork to mix together the almond milk, melted vegan butter, sugar, vanilla, baking powder and flax eggs. Mix in the oats, then fold in the rainbow sprinkles.

Pour the batter into the prepared casserole dish. Bake for 30 minutes, or until the oats are golden around the edges. Enjoy warm! Store leftovers in the fridge for up to 5 days.

TIP: Looking for a reduced-sugar option? Swap out the sugar for ½ cup (100 g) of monk fruit sweetener with erythritol. This will lower the calorie count to 141 per serving.

Jilly's Favorite Chewy Oatmeal Cookies

MAKES 24 cookies

ESTIMATED CALORIES:
112 per cookie
(without add-ins)

On my evenings in (when I'm not writing a book), I can frequently be found on my couch, munching on oatmeal cookies and watching Netflix. Nothing is more relaxing than cozying up with a tasty treat and a remote in hand! These oatmeal cookies are go-tos of mine because not only are they chewy and over-the-top delicious, they're super filling and a bit healthier than traditional oatmeal cookies. Flavored with cinnamon, sugar and a little maple syrup, these naturally gluten-free cookies are perfectly sweet and made in minutes. (See my tips to drive down the calories even more and boost the nutrition without sacrificing any of the flavor.) These 15-minute cookies are the perfect complement to your Netflix night in.

CLASSIC OATMEAL COOKIES

2 tbsp (20 g) flaxseed meal

¼ cup (60 ml) warm water

½ cup (120 ml) melted vegan butter or coconut oil (see Tips)

½ cup (100 g) coconut or cane sugar (see Tips)

¼ cup (60 ml) pure maple syrup

1 tbsp (15 ml) unsweetened almond milk

1 tsp vanilla extract

1 tsp ground cinnamon

1 tsp baking powder

¼ tsp salt

1 cup (125 g) oat flour (certified gluten-free, if needed)

2⅓ cups (209 g) quick oats (certified gluten-free, if needed)

TASTY OATMEAL COOKIE ADD-INS (OPTIONAL; CALORIES VARY)

¼ cup (36 g) raisins or dried cranberries

¼ cup (42 g) vegan chocolate chips

¼ cup (29 g) chopped nuts

Preheat the oven to 375°F (190°C). Line a baking sheet with parchment paper.

In a small bowl, mix the flaxseed meal with the warm water. Set aside for 2 minutes, or until a gel forms, to make flax eggs.

In a large bowl, use a fork to mix together the flax eggs, melted vegan butter, sugar, maple syrup, almond milk, vanilla, cinnamon, baking powder and salt. Then, add the oat flour and quick oats, and mix until a floppy, soft cookie dough forms. Fold in your add-ins or enjoy plain (my favorite)!

Use a tablespoon to scoop the cookie dough onto the prepared baking sheet, placing the dough portions about 1 inch (2.5 cm) apart. You should have about 24 cookies.

Bake for 10 minutes, or until the cookies lift easily off the paper and are lightly golden on the bottom. Remove from the oven, allow to cool and devour!

TIPS: Swap out the vegan butter for applesauce to shave off about 30 calories per cookie. Bring the count down a bit more by reducing the sugar: Use monk fruit sweetener with erythritol instead and you'll shave off another 15 calories, meaning you can enjoy these cookies for 67 calories a pop!

Flourless Oatmeal Brownies

SERVINGS: 12

ESTIMATED CALORIES:
164 per serving

This might be your new favorite way to make brownies. I like to call this chocolaty delicious treat my "Weekly Oatmeal Brownie Bake" because I shared this recipe with one of my best friends and now she makes it every single week! No one in her home is vegan and yet they gobble up this brownie bake within a day or two of baking. Everyone loves it, and no one can tell it's vegan and made without flour. This better-for-you oatmeal brownie is as easy to make as it is delicious. Plus, it's simple enough to bake during your busy weekdays. Curb your chocolate cravings anytime with this sweet brownie treat!

Nonstick spray, for casserole dish

1 cup (240 ml) unsweetened almond milk

½ cup (120 ml) melted vegan butter or coconut oil

1 cup (200 g) cane or coconut sugar, divided (see Tip)

½ cup (44 g) unsweetened cocoa powder (see Tip)

2 tsp (10 ml) vanilla extract

1 tsp baking powder

1½ cups (135 g) quick oats (certified gluten-free, if needed)

2 tbsp (22 g) vegan chocolate chips (optional)

Preheat the oven to 375°F (190°C). Spray a 9 x 11–inch (23 x 28–cm) casserole dish with nonstick spray.

In a medium-sized bowl, use a fork to mix together the almond milk, melted vegan butter, ¾ cup (150 g) of the sugar, cocoa powder, vanilla and baking powder. Add the quick oats and mix until incorporated.

Taste the batter for desired sweetness, and add some or all of the remaining ¼ cup (50 g) of sugar.

Pour the batter into the prepared casserole dish. Sprinkle the chocolate chips over the top (if using).

Bake for 25 to 30 minutes, or until completely risen in the center. Enjoy warm with a side of oat milk ice cream or coconut whipped cream.

> **TIP:** I've used as little as ½ cup (100 g) of sugar and ¼ cup (22 g) of cocoa powder in this and the results are just as delicious while being a little less sweet and lower calorie!

Make It Your Way Cookie Cake

SERVINGS: 16
ESTIMATED CALORIES: 165 per serving (unfrosted)

If you love cookie cake, you're going to go crazy over this easy, versatile, vegan cookie cake! It takes only about 30 minutes and the result is a super-moist, buttery and perfectly sweet treat that everyone will love. This recipe is a lower-calorie version of that kid-friendly bakery marvel and it's even more delicious than you can imagine. You will impress everyone with your baking skills when you serve this bad boy! Serve as a plain sugar cookie cake, in confetti sprinkle style, or add chocolate chips to make a chocolate chip cookie bake. I've also included my vanilla buttercream frosting for a festive topping.

COOKIE CAKE

Nonstick spray, for baking dish

¼ cup (40 g) flaxseed meal

½ cup (120 ml) warm water

1 cup (200 g) cane or coconut sugar

1 cup (240 ml) melted vegan butter

2 tsp (10 ml) unsweetened almond milk

2 tsp (10 ml) vanilla extract

2 tsp (9 g) baking powder

¼ tsp salt

1 cup (125 g) regular or gluten-free all-purpose flour (for gluten-free, I like King Arthur Gluten Free Measure for Measure)

1½ cups (135 g) quick oats (certified gluten-free, if needed; see Tip)

3 tbsp (36 g) rainbow sprinkles (optional; adds 9 calories per serving)

¼ cup (42 g) vegan chocolate chips (optional; adds 15 calories per serving)

VANILLA BUTTERCREAM FROSTING (OPTIONAL; ADDS 50 CALORIES PER SERVING)

1½ cups (180 g) confectioners' sugar

1 tbsp (14 g) softened vegan butter

1 tbsp (15 ml) unsweetened almond milk

1 tsp vanilla extract

Prepare the cookie cake: Preheat the oven to 375°F (190°C). Spray a 12-inch (30-cm) round baking dish with nonstick spray.

In a small bowl, mix the flaxseed meal with the warm water. Set aside for 2 minutes, or until a gel forms, to make flax eggs.

In a large bowl, use a fork to mix together the flax eggs, cane sugar, melted vegan butter, almond milk, vanilla, baking powder and salt. Then, add the flour and oats and mix until a thick batter forms. If your batter is still warm from being mixed, wait a couple of minutes to allow it to cool before gently folding in the rainbow sprinkles or chocolate chips (if using). Leave out the sprinkles or chocolate chips for a classic sugar cookie cake.

Transfer the batter to the prepared baking dish and use a spoon or silicone spatula to press it evenly into the dish. Bake for 20 to 25 minutes, or until the edges are golden and the cookie cake lifts easily from the dish. Allow the cake to cool before frosting.

This cake is perfectly sweet with or without the frosting. To make the buttercream frosting: In a medium-sized bowl, combine the confectioners' sugar, vegan butter, almond milk and vanilla, and beat with an electric mixer until smooth. Use a pastry bag or resealable plastic bag (snip a corner off) to pipe the frosting around the edges of the cake once it has cooled. Cut into 16 slices and serve.

LOWER CALORIE SWAPS: Use as little as ¾ cup (150 g) of sugar and ¾ cup (180 ml) of melted vegan butter in this recipe for 140 calories per serving.

TIP: No oats? No problem. Use an additional 1 cup (125 g) of regular or gluten-free all-purpose flour in place of the quick oats in this recipe! This adds 15 calories per serving.

Ooey-Gooey Cocoa-Banana Brownies

MAKES
12 brownies

ESTIMATED CALORIES:
88 per brownie
made with monk
fruit / 101 per
brownie made
with sugar

In the mood for a healthier version of intensely chocolaty, ooey-gooey brownies? Give these yummy brownies a go! They are unbelievably moist, rich and chocolaty. Y'all, they melt in your mouth! This recipe is so easy to make, and you won't believe how low calorie it is. Imagine a brownie and banana bread joining forces. Everybody is going to love these—no one will believe they're around 100 calories a pop and everyone will be back for seconds.

Nonstick spray, for baking dish

2 overripe bananas, mashed

¼ cup (60 ml) melted vegan butter or coconut oil

⅔ cup (133 g) monk fruit sweetener with erythritol, or ¾ cup (150 g) cane or coconut sugar

⅓ cup (80 ml) unsweetened almond milk

1 tsp vanilla extract

1 tsp baking powder

¼ tsp salt

½ cup (44 g) good-quality unsweetened cocoa powder

½ cup (63 g) regular or gluten-free all-purpose flour (for gluten-free, I like King Arthur Gluten Free Measure for Measure)

2 tbsp (22 g) vegan chocolate chips

Preheat the oven to 350°F (175°C). Spray a 10- to 12-inch (25- to 30-cm) baking dish with nonstick spray.

In a medium-sized bowl, use a fork to mix together the bananas, melted vegan butter, monk fruit sweetener, almond milk, vanilla, baking powder and salt. Add the cocoa powder and mix until combined. Add the flour and mix until creamy.

Spoon the batter into the prepared dish and sprinkle the chocolate chips on top.

Bake for 20 to 25 minutes, or until baked around the edges. Remove from the oven and allow to cool for about 5 minutes before cutting into 12 pieces and sinking your teeth into some intense chocolaty goodness! These are amazing with a scoop of oat milk ice cream.

Sweet and Salty Trail Mix Cookies

MAKES 18 cookies
ESTIMATED CALORIES:
118 per cookie

Did you grow up munching on trail mix, as I did? You know the kind—handfuls of peanuts, pretzels and pieces of chocolate. It always seemed to curb my sweet and salty cravings in one bite. Imagine that healthy snack, baked into a cookie! These are almost too delicious: chewy, moist and soft, with crisp and savory pretzels baked in. They are drizzled with chocolate and peanut butter—and the result is the perfect treat to satisfy your salty and crunchy hankering and your sweet tooth at the same time!

2 tbsp (20 g) flaxseed meal

¼ cup (60 ml) warm water

½ cup (120 ml) melted vegan butter

2 tbsp (30 ml) pure maple syrup

1 tsp vanilla extract

1 tsp unsweetened almond milk

1 tsp baking powder

¼ tsp cane sugar

½ tsp salt

1¼ cups (156 g) regular or gluten-free all-purpose flour (for gluten-free, I like King Arthur Gluten Free Measure for Measure)

18 regular or gluten-free salted or unsalted mini pretzels

¼ cup (60 ml) melted peanut butter (melt in a microwave)

¼ cup (60 ml) melted vegan chocolate chips (melt in a microwave)

Sea salt flakes, for sprinkling

Preheat the oven to 425°F (220°C). Line a baking sheet with parchment paper.

In a small bowl, mix the flaxseed meal with the warm water. Set aside for 2 minutes, or until a gel forms, to make flax eggs.

In a medium-sized bowl, use a fork to mix together the flax eggs, melted vegan butter, maple syrup, vanilla, almond milk, baking powder, sugar and salt. Then, mix in the flour until a thick cookie dough forms.

Use your hands to roll the dough into 18 balls and then place them on the prepared baking sheet, spacing them about 1½ inches (4 cm) apart.

Use two fingers to press the cookie dough balls to about ⅓-inch (1-cm) thickness and then gently press a mini pretzel into the top of each cookie. Bake for 10 minutes, or until the cookies are golden around the edges and lift easily off the parchment paper.

Allow the cookies to cool, then drizzle with the melted peanut butter and chocolate and top with sea salt. Enjoy!

HEALTHY OAT FLOUR SWAP: Substitute the 1¼ cups (156 g) regular or gluten-free all-purpose flour with 2 cups (250 g) oat flour. This adds 16 calories per cookie.

IRRESISTIBLE CUPCAKES AND CAKES

Welcome to the heart of this better-for-you vegan baking book. Here, you will find lighter versions of my most favorite indulgent recipes. You will see that it is possible to make delicious crowd-pleasing cakes and cupcakes without eggs or dairy. Every recipe can be made gluten-free, comes together in minutes and uses simple and affordable ingredients. Never baked a cake before? No problem—my straightforward instructions are easy enough for anyone to follow! And, since they're lower calorie, you can have your cake and eat a few slices, too!

My inspiration in this chapter came from my memories of enjoying sweet treats with the ones I love. Whether we're talking about Dad's Light Key Lime Bundt Cake (page 55), sinking our teeth into some Double Chocolate Banana Cupcakes (page 47) or whipping up my 25-Minute Strawberry Sheet Pan Cake (page 48) that reminds me of Mom, I've baked my little vegan heart right into each deliciously satisfying low-cal vegan bite of cake. I've served each of these recipes to nonvegans and vegans alike and they are always crowd-pleasers. Don't take my word for it—let's bake something sweet!

Any Occasion Vanilla Cupcakes and Cake

SERVINGS:
16 (cupcakes) /
12 (cake)

ESTIMATED CALORIES:
129 per unfrosted
cupcake / 179 per
unfrosted cake slice

Need a treat to bring to a special occasion? Vanilla cupcakes are always a favorite, and you may want to make an extra batch of these because they will go fast! They're fluffy, moist and sweet, and ready to be decorated with colorful sprinkles that match the occasion.

PERFECT VANILLA CUPCAKES

1¼ cups (300 ml) unsweetened almond milk

1 cup (200 g) cane sugar (see Tip)

¼ cup (60 ml) melted vegan butter

1½ tsp (7 g) baking powder

1 tsp baking soda

1 tsp vanilla extract

2 cups (250 g) regular or gluten-free all-purpose flour (for gluten-free, I like King Arthur Gluten Free Measure for Measure)

¼ cup (48 g) rainbow sprinkles (optional)

PERFECT VANILLA CAKE

Nonstick spray, for pan

1 cup (240 ml) unsweetened almond milk

¾ cup (150 g) cane sugar

⅓ cup (80 ml) melted vegan butter

1½ tsp (7 g) baking powder

1 tsp baking soda

1 tsp vanilla extract

1¾ cups (219 g) regular or gluten-free all-purpose flour (for gluten-free, I like King Arthur Gluten Free Measure for Measure)

¼ cup (48 g) rainbow sprinkles (optional)

VANILLA BUTTERCREAM FROSTING (ADDS 100 CALORIES PER CUPCAKE AND 66 CALORIES PER CAKE SLICE)

3 cups (360 g) confectioners' sugar

2 tbsp (28 g) softened vegan butter

2 tbsp (30 ml) unsweetened almond milk

1 tsp vanilla extract

Prepare the cupcakes or cake: Preheat the oven to 350°F (175°C) and line 16 wells of a muffin pan or spray an 8- to 10-inch (20- to 25-cm) round cake pan with nonstick spray. For a loaf cake, preheat the oven to 375°F (190°C) and spray a 9 x 5–inch (23 x 13–cm) loaf pan with nonstick spray.

In a large bowl, use a fork or whisk to mix together the almond milk, cane sugar, melted vegan butter, baking powder, baking soda and vanilla. Then, add the flour and mix just until a smooth batter forms. Make funfetti-style cupcakes or cake by folding the sprinkles directly into the batter, if desired.

Spoon the batter into the lined muffin pan or pour the batter into the prepared round cake pan or loaf pan. Bake for 25 to 30 minutes, or until the top of the cupcakes or cake are lightly golden. If baking a full cake, you may need to bake for an additional 5 to 10 minutes. Test the center of the cake with a toothpick to see if it comes out clean—your signal that it's done.

Prepare the buttercream frosting: In a medium-sized bowl, use an electric hand mixer to mix together the confectioners' sugar, softened vegan butter, almond milk and vanilla. Note that for a loaf cake, you will only need half of the frosting; either divide the ingredients in half or make the entire frosting recipe and freeze the remaining frosting to use at a later time.

Remove the cupcakes or cake from the oven, remove from the pan and let cool completely on a wire rack before frosting. I find these cupcakes delicious with or without frosting.

TIP: Want a 109-calorie cupcake without icing? Use ¼ cup (50 g) of sugar plus 4 teaspoons (10 g) of pure powdered stevia in place of the full cup of cane sugar for perfectly sweet vanilla cupcakes.

The Ultimate Chocolate Chip Cookie Cake

SERVINGS: 16
ESTIMATED CALORIES: 161 per serving (without icing)

Imagine the soft fluffy texture of a perfect slice of cake and the buttery sweet flavor of a chocolate chip cookie combined in each bite. The moment I created this recipe, I knew it would be a showstopper. This is one of the easiest cakes you'll ever bake and it's melt-in-your-mouth good! Everybody you serve this to is going to love it and beg you for the recipe. Sweetened with maple syrup, loaded with chocolate chips in every bite, super moist and buttery—this cake will put a smile on everyone's face. No eggs, no dairy and no refined sugar—just an incredibly scrumptious and tender chocolate chip cake that is perfect for any occasion.

. . . .

COOKIE CAKE

Nonstick spray, for pan

1 cup (240 ml) unsweetened almond milk

⅓ cup (80 ml) melted vegan butter

1 cup (240 ml) pure maple syrup

1 tsp vanilla extract

1½ tsp (7 g) baking powder

1 tsp baking soda

1¾ cups (219 g) regular or gluten-free all-purpose flour (for gluten-free, I like King Arthur Gluten Free Measure for Measure)

¼ cup (42 g) vegan chocolate chips

VANILLA ICING (ADDS 28 CALORIES PER SERVING)

¾ cup (90 g) confectioners' sugar

1 tbsp (14 g) softened vegan butter

1 tbsp (15 ml) unsweetened almond milk

1 tsp vanilla extract

Prepare the cookie cake: Preheat the oven to 375°F (190°C) and spray an 8- to 10-inch (20- to 25-cm) round cake pan with cooking spray.

In a medium-sized bowl, use a fork to mix together the almond milk, melted vegan butter, maple syrup, vanilla, baking powder and baking soda. Then, mix in the flour until a smooth batter forms. Fold in the chocolate chips.

Pour the batter into the prepared cake pan and bake for 30 to 35 minutes, or until lightly golden on top.

While the cake bakes, prepare the vanilla icing: In a medium-sized bowl, use an electric hand mixer to mix together the confectioners' sugar, softened vegan butter, almond milk and vanilla.

Remove the cake from the oven and allow it to cool in the pan or remove from the pan and let cool on a wire rack before drizzling it with the icing.

Southern-Style Apple Cake with Cinnamon Cream Cheese Frosting

SERVINGS: 12
ESTIMATED CALORIES:
198 per serving
(unfrosted)

One of my North Carolina friends turned me on to apple cake, and my mouth waters just thinking about it! I set out to create a healthier vegan version that is just as moist, tender and delicious as the "real thing." Now, I bake this for friends and family every chance I get—and everyone who has ever tried a slice has told me that it's one of the best cakes they've ever had! The combination of the buttery texture, sweet maple cinnamon and incredible apple flavor baked into a homemade cake is out of this world. Top it with this finger-licking good cinnamon cream cheese frosting—you'll be in southern-style heaven! My secret to the velvety and moist texture of this healthier vegan and gluten-free cake is the oats and oat flour.

APPLE CAKE

Nonstick spray, for pan

1 cup (240 ml) unsweetened applesauce

¾ cup (180 ml) pure maple syrup

½ cup (120 ml) melted vegan butter

½ cup (120 ml) unsweetened almond milk

1 tsp vanilla extract

2 tsp (9 g) baking powder

2 tsp (9 g) baking soda

1 tsp ground cinnamon

½ cup (45 g) quick oats (certified gluten-free, if needed)

2¼ cups (281 g) oat flour (certified gluten-free, if needed)

CINNAMON CREAM CHEESE FROSTING (OPTIONAL; ADDS 75 CALORIES PER SERVING)

2 oz (57 g) vegan cream cheese

2 tbsp (28 g) softened vegan butter

¾ cup (90 g) confectioners' sugar

½ tsp ground cinnamon

Prepare the apple cake: Preheat the oven to 375°F (190°C). Spray a 9 x 5–inch (23 x 13–cm) loaf pan with nonstick spray.

In a large bowl, use a fork or whisk to mix together the applesauce, maple syrup, melted vegan butter, almond milk, vanilla, baking powder, baking soda and cinnamon. Add the oats and oat flour and mix until well combined.

Pour the batter into the prepared loaf pan. Bake for 40 to 50 minutes, or until you can stick a toothpick into the center of the cake and it comes out clean.

Prepare the cinnamon cream cheese frosting (if using): In a medium-sized bowl, use an electric mixer to mix together the vegan cream cheese, softened vegan butter, confectioners' sugar and cinnamon.

Once the apple cake is done, remove it from the oven and its pan. Slice and serve warm. I love enjoying it this way with a little softened vegan butter spread over the top. My mom loves drizzling maple syrup over it!

If frosting, allow the cake to cool on a wire rack, then spread with the cinnamon cream cheese frosting.

Double Chocolate Banana Cupcakes

MAKES 14 to 16 cupcakes

ESTIMATED CALORIES: 168 per cupcake (without icing)

If you like my Any Occasion Vanilla Cupcakes (page 40), you're going to love this chocolaty banana version! Just like their vanilla cousin, these cupcakes are as simple to make as they are delicious! Both cupcakes are fantastically sweet, even without icing. And, as for the vanilla cupcakes, there also is a reduced-sugar version (see tip) that is just as yummy. I double up on the chocolate in this recipe to give you chocolate lovers a mind-blowing cupcake experience. Top them with delicious chocolate frosting and you've got a new family-favorite recipe everyone will beg for!

. . . .

CHOCOLATE CUPCAKES

1 cup (240 ml) unsweetened almond milk

3 cups (124 g) ripe bananas, mashed

¾ cup (180 ml) maple syrup

½ cup (120 ml) melted vegan butter or coconut oil

2 tsp (9 g) baking powder

1 tsp baking soda

1 tsp vanilla extract

¼ cup (22 g) cocoa powder

2 cups (250 g) regular or gluten-free all-purpose flour (for gluten-free, I like King Arthur Gluten Free Measure for Measure)

¼ cup (42 g) mini vegan chocolate chips

CHOCOLATE FROSTING (ADDS 50 CALORIES PER SERVING)

1½ cups (180 g) confectioners' sugar

2 tbsp (28 g) softened vegan butter

3 tbsp (15 g) cocoa powder

2 tbsp (30 ml) unsweetened almond milk

1 tsp vanilla extract

2 tbsp (24 g) rainbow sprinkles

Prepare the cupcakes: Preheat the oven to 350°F (175°C). Line 14 to 16 wells of a cupcake pan.

In a large bowl, use a fork or whisk to mix together the almond milk, mashed bananas, maple syrup, melted vegan butter, baking powder, baking soda and vanilla. Then, add the cocoa powder and mix until completely combined. Mix in the flour just until the batter is smooth. Fold in the vegan chocolate chips.

Pour the batter into the lined cupcake wells. Bake for 25 minutes, or until they have completely risen.

While the cupcakes bake, make the chocolate icing: In a medium-sized bowl, use an electric hand mixer to mix together the confectioners' sugar, softened vegan butter, cocoa powder, almond milk and vanilla.

Remove the cupcakes from the oven and allow them to cool, then spoon the chocolate frosting over the top. Top with the rainbow sprinkles.

These store well for up to 3 days in an airtight container at room temperature.

HEALTHY OAT FLOUR SWAP: Substitute the 2 cups (250 g) regular or gluten-free all-purpose flour with 2½ cups (313 g) oat flour. This adds 14 calories per cupcake.

25-Minute Strawberry Sheet Pan Cake

SERVINGS: 16

ESTIMATED CALORIES: 158 per serving (without icing)

When I was a kid, my mom used to buy mini angel food cakes and fresh strawberries from the grocery store bakery. She'd bring them home and then immediately soak the strawberries in sugar. After about 30 minutes, we'd use them as a topping on our little cakes with whipped cream. Okay, so this wasn't vegan—but my recipe is, and it tastes even better and is better for you! This sheet pan cake is so moist that it actually melts in your mouth, and the sugary berries are the perfect topping. At under 200 calories per slice, this is going to be a go-to sweet for you and your family.

. . . .

SHEET PAN CAKE

2 cups (332 g) whole or sliced fresh or frozen strawberries, divided

¼ cup (50 g) coconut or cane sugar

Nonstick spray, for pan

1 cup (240 ml) unsweetened almond milk

¾ cup (180 ml) pure maple syrup

½ cup (120 ml) melted vegan butter

2 tsp (10 ml) vanilla extract

1½ tsp (7 g) baking powder

1 tsp baking soda

2 cups (250 g) regular or gluten-free all-purpose flour (for gluten-free, I like King Arthur Gluten Free Measure for Measure)

VANILLA ICING (OPTIONAL; ADDS 25 CALORIES PER SERVING)

1 cup (120 g) confectioners' sugar

2 tbsp (30 ml) unsweetened almond milk

1 tsp vanilla extract

Prepare the sheet pan cake: Place 1 cup (166 g) of the strawberries in a small bowl and toss them in the coconut sugar. Set aside or refrigerate for at least 30 minutes.

Preheat the oven to 375°F (190°C). Spray a rimmed baking sheet with nonstick spray.

In a large bowl, use a fork or whisk to mix together the almond milk, maple syrup, melted vegan butter, vanilla, baking powder and baking soda. Mix in the flour until the batter is smooth, then fold in the remaining cup (166 g) of strawberries.

Pour the batter onto the prepared baking sheet and bake for 25 minutes, or until golden.

While the cake bakes, prepare the icing (if using): In a medium-sized bowl, use a whisk to mix together the confectioners' sugar, almond milk and vanilla until smooth. Set aside.

When the cake is done, remove it from the oven and allow it to cool completely in its pan before drizzling the icing (if using) over the top. You may remove the cake from the pan and serve it on a platter or slice and serve it directly from the pan, with the sugared berries spooned over the top.

Banana Lovers' Cake with Banana Cream Cheese Glaze

SERVINGS: 16
ESTIMATED CALORIES: 232 per serving (without glaze)

Do you know anyone who loves bananas in almost anything? I've got a few people in mind—and I'm one of them! My mouth is watering just thinking about this buttery banana cake. If you like my Must-Try Banana Bread (page 80), this recipe is going to knock your banana-lovin' socks off! Banana cake is kind of like banana bread, but even more moist and sweet. It's fantastic served on its own and even better topped with my easy homemade banana cream cheese glaze. You'll want to lick that glaze right off the spoon. Trust me . . . I've done it.

BANANA LOVERS' CAKE

Nonstick spray, for pan

3 overripe bananas, mashed

1½ cups (360 ml) unsweetened almond milk

2 tbsp (30 ml) fresh lemon juice

½ cup (120 ml) melted vegan butter

¾ cup (150 g) coconut sugar

½ cup (120 ml) pure maple syrup

2 tsp (9 g) baking powder

1 tsp baking soda

1 tsp vanilla extract

1 tsp ground cinnamon

3 cups (375 g) regular or gluten-free all-purpose flour (for gluten-free, I like King Arthur Gluten Free Measure for Measure)

BANANA CREAM CHEESE GLAZE (ADDS 38 CALORIES PER SERVING)

1 overripe banana, mashed

2 tbsp (28 g) softened vegan butter

2 oz (57 g) vegan cream cheese

1 cup (120 g) confectioners' sugar

1 tsp vanilla extract

½ tsp fresh lemon juice

Prepare the banana cake: Preheat the oven to 350°F (175°C). Spray a 9-inch (23-cm) round springform pan with nonstick spray.

In a large bowl, use a fork or whisk to mix together the bananas, almond milk, lemon juice, melted vegan butter, coconut sugar, maple syrup, baking powder, baking soda, vanilla and cinnamon. Then, mix in the flour until a smooth batter forms.

Pour the batter into the prepared springform pan. Bake for 35 to 40 minutes. Test the cake for doneness by inserting a toothpick into the center to ensure it comes out clean.

While the cake bakes, prepare the banana cream cheese glaze: In a medium-sized bowl, use an electric hand mixer to mix together the banana, softened vegan butter, vegan cream cheese, confectioners' sugar, vanilla and lemon juice. Set aside until ready to serve.

Remove the cake from the oven and from the pan, and allow it to cool on a wire rack. Enjoy warm, spread with the glaze.

Peanut Butter and Jelly Cupcakes

MAKES
18 cupcakes
ESTIMATED CALORIES:
174 per cupcake

PB&J fans, your childhood dreams have come true! Peanut Butter and Jilly is the name of my blog and it probably won't surprise you to hear that I love PB&J! Guys, these jelly-filled peanut butter cupcakes are my jam! If you yearn for the nostalgic flavor of peanut butter and jelly, these cupcakes will satisfy that craving. Using peanut butter powder keeps them on the lighter side—all the flavor without the fat! Use low-calorie jam and you won't notice the difference when you sink your teeth into one of these. Don't let that low calorie count fool ya; these taste even more indulgent than they look.

2 tbsp (20 g) flaxseed meal

¼ cup (60 ml) warm water

1¼ cups (300 ml) unsweetened almond milk

¾ cup (180 ml) pure maple syrup

⅓ cup (80 ml) melted vegan butter

1 tsp vanilla extract

1 tsp baking powder

1 tsp baking soda

1 tsp ground cinnamon

⅓ cup (80 g) peanut butter powder

2 cups (250 g) regular or gluten-free all-purpose flour (for gluten-free, I like King Arthur Gluten Free Measure for Measure)

6 tbsp (80 ml) low-calorie jam of your choice (calories vary; I used Trader Joe's Reduced Sugar Organic Strawberry Preserves)

Peanut butter, for topping (optional; calories vary)

Preheat the oven to 350°F (175°C). Line 18 wells of a muffin pan.

In a small bowl, mix together the flaxseed meal with the warm water. Set aside for 2 minutes, or until a gel forms, to make flax eggs.

In a large bowl, use a fork to mix together the flax eggs, almond milk, maple syrup, melted vegan butter, vanilla, baking powder, baking soda and cinnamon. Next, add the peanut butter powder and mix until combined. Then, add the flour and mix until a smooth batter forms.

Fill the prepared muffin wells one-third of the way with batter. Drop a teaspoon of the jam into the center of each portion of muffin batter. Spoon the remaining batter over the jelly so that each muffin well is filled about two-thirds of the way full. Bake for about 30 minutes, or until the cupcakes have completely risen and are lightly golden.

Remove the cupcakes from the oven and serve them warm or cooled. If you desire, spread the peanut butter on top.

Dad's Light Key Lime Bundt Cake

This lime cake is inspired by my dear dad, the lover of all things Key lime. This cake will teleport you into paradise and you'll be singing "Margaritaville" like my dad in no time. This simple and easy Bundt cake is citrusy, moist and tender . . . never mind that it's vegan, gluten-free optional and takes only minutes. I've included vegan cream cheese frosting or a skinny lime glaze to top this tasty treat. For those watching their waistline before diving into a slice of paradise, use my reduced sugar swap (see Tip).

SERVINGS: 16
ESTIMATED CALORIES: 149 per serving (including glaze)

LIGHT KEY LIME BUNDT CAKE

Nonstick spray, for pan

1 cup (240 ml) unsweetened almond milk

¼ cup (60 ml) melted vegan butter

½ cup (120 ml) fresh lime juice

¾ cup (150 g) cane sugar (see Tip)

1½ tsp (/ g) baking powder

1 tsp baking soda

2 tsp (10 ml) vanilla extract

2¼ cups (281 g) regular or gluten-free all-purpose flour (for gluten-free, I like King Arthur Gluten Free Measure for Measure)

LIME GLAZE

¾ cup (90 g) confectioners' sugar

1 tbsp (15 ml) unsweetened almond milk, plus more for thinning

1 tbsp (15 ml) fresh lime juice

1 tsp vanilla extract

Prepare the lime cake: Preheat the oven to 375°F (190°C). Spray a Bundt cake pan with nonstick spray. Alternatively, you may bake this in a 9 x 5–inch (23 x 13–cm) loaf pan or 9-inch (23-cm) round cake pan, which should be prepared the same way.

In a large bowl, use a fork or whisk to mix together the almond milk, melted vegan butter, lime juice, cane sugar, baking powder, baking soda and vanilla. The mixture will begin to bubble. Quickly add the flour and mix until a smooth batter forms. Be careful not to overmix the batter, or else the cake will become tough.

Pour the batter into the prepared pan. Bake for about 40 minutes, or until the cake has completely risen and is lightly golden.

While the cake bakes, prepare the lime glaze: In a small bowl, use a whisk or hand mixer to mix together the confectioners' sugar, almond milk, lime juice and vanilla until smooth, adding a little more almond milk if necessary to reach the right consistency for drizzling.

When the cake is done, remove it from the oven, allow the cake to cool in the pan, then remove from the pan. Drizzle the lime glaze over the top or enjoy without icing for an even lighter slice!

TIP: Make this cake even lighter by using ¼ cup (50 g) of cane sugar plus 4 teaspoons (10 g) of pure powdered stevia in place of the ¾ cup (150 g) of sugar. The result is only 109 calories per slice.

TOPPING SWAP: This cake is delicious with or without the vegan lime glaze. If you're in the mood for something creamier, it also tastes amazing with my famous vegan cream cheese frosting: Just whip together 1½ cups (180 g) of confectioners' sugar, ¼ cup (57 g) of vegan cream cheese and ¼ cup (57 g) of softened vegan butter. This adds about 40 calories per slice.

Perfectly Portioned Chocolate Cakes

SERVINGS: 16
ESTIMATED CALORIES: 141 per serving (including frosting)

When I was a kid, my favorite part of the grocery store was the aisle that held all of the pre-packaged desserts and cakes. You know the place—the bagged mini muffins, the boxed cupcakes, the sticky buns . . . They used to hit the spot as a kid, but as an adult, I prefer something homemade with a cleaner ingredient list. These vegan chocolate mini cakes are perfectly portioned, just like the boxed snack cakes you remember. They're made with better-for-you ingredients and contain no dairy or eggs! I top them with a creamy vegan vanilla frosting, but I've also been known to drizzle these with melted vegan chocolate or eat them plain. Everyone is going to love sinking their teeth into these kid-friendly chocolate treats.

MINI CHOCOLATE CAKES

Nonstick spray, for pans

1½ cups (360 ml) unsweetened almond milk

½ cup (120 ml) melted vegan butter or coconut oil

¾ cup (150 g) cane or coconut sugar

1 tsp vanilla extract

1 tsp baking soda

1 tsp baking powder

⅓ cup (29 g) unsweetened cocoa powder

2 cups (250 g) regular or gluten-free all-purpose flour (for gluten-free, I like King Arthur Gluten Free Measure for Measure)

VEGAN VANILLA FROSTING

1½ cups (180 g) confectioners' sugar

2 tbsp (30 ml) unsweetened almond milk

1 tbsp (14 g) softened vegan butter

1 tsp vanilla extract

Prepare the mini chocolate cakes: Preheat the oven to 350°F (175°C). Spray 16 silicone whoopie pie pans, mini cake pans, cupcake wells or ramekins with nonstick spray.

In a large bowl, mix together the almond milk, melted vegan butter, cane sugar, vanilla, baking soda, baking powder and cocoa powder. Then, add the flour and mix until a smooth batter is formed.

Pour the batter into your prepared molds. Bake for 20 to 25 minutes, or until the cakes have completely risen and you can stick a toothpick into the center of a cake and it comes out clean.

While the cakes bake, prepare the vegan vanilla frosting: In a medium-sized bowl, use an electric hand mixer to mix together the confectioners' sugar, almond milk, softened vegan butter and vanilla.

Remove the cakes from their molds and place on your serving dish. Allow them to cool, then drizzle them with the vegan vanilla frosting.

Rich Red Velvet Cake with Cream Cheese Frosting

SERVINGS: 12
ESTIMATED CALORIES: 206 per serving (unfrosted)

Whether it's for a birthday, the holiday season or Valentine's Day, or you're just in the mood for some good old-fashioned red velvet cake—you're going to love this cake! This veganized version of a well-known decadent dessert is everything a red velvet cake should be. "Red velvet" is the perfect way to describe this cake because the texture is just that . . . velvety. And that rich red color makes it all the more indulgent. The best part is the vegan cream cheese frosting spread on top. If you have any red velvet lovers in your crew, a slice of this cake will satisfy their sweet tooth. They'll think you spent hours in the kitchen (when you spent only minutes) and they will never guess it's vegan.

RED VELVET CAKE

Nonstick spray, for pan

1¼ cups (300 ml) unsweetened almond milk

½ cup (120 ml) melted vegan butter

1 cup (200 g) cane sugar (see Tip)

¼ cup (22 g) unsweetened cocoa powder

1 tsp vanilla extract

1½ tsp (7 g) baking powder

1 tsp baking soda

5 tsp (25 ml) red food coloring

2 cups (250 g) regular or gluten-free all-purpose flour (for gluten-free, I like King Arthur Gluten Free Measure for Measure)

Red sprinkles (optional; calories vary)

VEGAN CREAM CHEESE FROSTING (ADDS 75 CALORIES PER SERVING)

1½ cups (180 g) confectioners' sugar

2 oz (57 g) vegan cream cheese

¼ cup (57 g) softened vegan butter

Prepare the cake: Preheat the oven to 375°F (190°C). Spray a 9 x 5–inch (23 x 13–cm) loaf pan or an 8- to 9-inch (20- to 23-cm) round cake pan with nonstick spray.

In a large bowl, use a fork or whisk to mix together the almond milk, melted vegan butter, cane sugar, cocoa powder, vanilla, baking powder and baking soda. Next, mix in the red food coloring. Then, mix in the flour until a smooth batter is formed.

Pour the cake batter into the prepared pan. Bake for 40 minutes for a loaf or 30 minutes for a round cake. You will know it's done when you can stick a toothpick into the center of the cake and it comes out clean.

While the cake bakes, prepare the vegan cream cheese frosting: In a medium-sized bowl, use an electric mixer to mix together the confectioners' sugar, vegan cream cheese and softened vegan butter.

Remove the cake from the pan and place it on your serving dish. Allow it to cool before spreading the frosting over the top. Top with the red sprinkles or enjoy as is!

TIP: Swap the 1 cup (200 g) cane sugar for ¼ cup (50 g) plus 5 teaspoons (13 g) pure powdered stevia. This will result in a 156 calorie slice (unfrosted).

LIGHTER FROSTING OPTION: Instead of spreading the entire batch of frosting over the cake, use half and drizzle it over the top once the cake has cooled, adding only about 35 calories per slice. You may store the remaining frosting in the fridge for up to 3 days or the freezer for up to 30 days.

Nut-Free Vanilla Cheesecake

SERVINGS: 16
ESTIMATED CALORIES:
121 per serving

Cheesecake is the ultimate creamy indulgence—and now you can enjoy it even on a plant-based diet or while you're watching your waistline! If you've been around the vegan block, you may have seen a cashew cheesecake before. And, while cashew cheesecake is delicious, and cashews are super healthy, they are also high in calories. This version is a naturally gluten-free, nut-free, lighter and better-for-you option! Its delicious and buttery cinnamon-sugar piecrust is out of this world, and don't even get me started on the creamy vegan New York–style cheesecake filling! Bake it into one large cheesecake or mini cheesecakes. Serve this to your friends and family—everyone will be licking their plates clean!

. . . .

CINNAMON SUGAR OATMEAL PIECRUST

Nonstick spray, for pan(s)

½ cup (100 g) cane or coconut sugar

⅓ cup (80 ml) unsweetened applesauce

¼ cup (60 ml) melted coconut oil or vegan butter

1 tsp ground cinnamon

1 cup (90 g) quick oats (certified gluten-free, if needed)

¼ cup (31 g) oat flour (certified gluten-free, if needed) or regular all-purpose flour

VEGAN NUT-FREE CHEESECAKE FILLING

12 oz (340 g) vegan cream cheese

9 oz (255 g) vegan coconut whipped cream

1 cup (120 g) confectioners' sugar

¼ cup (32 g) cornstarch

1 tbsp (15 ml) fresh lemon juice

2 tsp (10 ml) vanilla extract

Prepare the piecrust: Preheat the oven to 350°F (175°C). Spray eight mini springform pans or an 8- to 9-inch (20- to 23-cm) springform pan with nonstick spray.

In a medium-sized bowl, use a fork or whisk to mix together the cane sugar, applesauce, melted coconut oil, cinnamon, quick oats and oat flour. Press the crust mixture evenly into the prepared pan(s).

Prepare the filling: In a large bowl, use an electric mixer to mix together the vegan cream cheese, coconut whipped cream, confectioners' sugar, cornstarch, lemon juice and vanilla.

Pour the filling mixture evenly over the crust and bake for about 40 minutes, or until the cheesecake is lightly golden around the edges. Remove the cheesecake from the oven and allow it to cool, then cover and refrigerate it for 2 hours (or preferably overnight) before serving. Enjoy this dessert plain or topped with your favorite berries.

EASY, HEALTHY PIES, COBBLERS AND CRISPS

If cakes were the heart of this vegan baking book, this comforting and crave-worthy chapter is the soul. I'm a southern girl and I couldn't write a baking book without including my favorite pies, cobblers and bakes. Here, you will find recipes that are lighter takes on the stick-to-your-ribs recipes that I grew up loving. From homestyle pies, cozy cobblers and crisps, each recipe is lighter, surprisingly healthy and easy enough for anyone to follow. They also require simple ingredients that you probably already have on hand.

Nothing tastes like home more than the 8-Ingredient Cherry Pie Oatmeal (page 71), a healthy vegan and gluten-free spin on cherry pie that will become a go-to breakfast or dessert for you. My 30-Minute Homestyle Blueberry Pie (page 64) is quite literally one of the best things you'll ever eat. And the chapter wouldn't be complete without a low-calorie, better-for-you, vegan version of my aunt's famous Craving Peach Cobbler (page 75). Imagine the sweet aroma of a pie or cobbler baking in your oven. And remember—it's all more nutritious, vegan and delicious! You won't believe how easy it is to serve up a slice of one of these homemade pies or bakes.

30-Minute Homestyle Blueberry Pie

SERVINGS: 12
ESTIMATED CALORIES: 216 per serving

There's just something about a homemade pie coming out of the oven, hot and ready to be sliced. Pies can be intimidating for some people, but this one is so easy that anyone can do it! This comforting blueberry pie is made in a fraction of the time it takes to bake a traditional pie at home, and with a fraction of the calories. It starts with my simple homemade filling made in less than 10 minutes. We bake it within an easy-to-make buttery, golden piecrust. The result is an irresistible pie loaded with bubbling blueberries that will make your home smell amazing! Everyone's tummy will be happy and they'll definitely go back for seconds.

10-MINUTE BLUEBERRY PIE FILLING

1 tbsp (14 g) vegan butter or coconut oil

4 cups (592 g) fresh or frozen blueberries

¼ cup (50 g) cane sugar

2 tbsp (30 ml) fresh lemon juice

1 tsp vanilla extract

½ tsp ground cinnamon

¼ cup (31 g) regular or gluten-free all-purpose flour (for gluten-free, I like King Arthur Gluten Free Measure for Measure)

¼ cup (32 g) cornstarch

5-INGREDIENT PIECRUST

Nonstick spray, for pie dish

¾ cup (180 ml) unsweetened almond milk

½ cup (120 ml) melted vegan butter

1 tbsp (15 ml) pure maple syrup

1½ tsp (7 g) baking powder

2 cups (250 g) regular or gluten-free all-purpose flour (for gluten-free, I like King Arthur Gluten Free Measure for Measure)

Prepare the blueberry pie filling: Melt the vegan butter in a medium-sized saucepan over medium heat. Add the blueberries, sugar, lemon juice, vanilla and cinnamon. Cook, stirring, for 5 to 7 minutes, or until the berries begin to bubble; if you use frozen berries, this may take longer. Remove them from the heat and whisk in the flour and cornstarch. Set aside to cool.

Prepare the piecrust: Spray a 9- to 11-inch (23- to 28-cm) pie dish with nonstick spray and set aside.

In a medium-sized bowl, use a fork or whisk to mix together the almond milk, melted vegan butter, maple syrup and baking powder. Then, add the flour and mix until a thick dough forms. Divide the dough into two equal portions.

Place one portion of the dough on a floured surface and use a rolling pin to roll it into a 10- to 12-inch (25- to 30-cm)-diameter round. Place the dough round in the prepared pie dish, using your hands to press it into and along the edges of the dish. Roll out the second portion of dough in the same manner.

Pour the blueberry pie filling evenly into the dough-lined dish. Cover it with the second dough round. Use your hands to join the bottom and top rounds all along the circumference of the dish, ensuring the edge is sealed and covers the edge of the dish. Use a knife to slice several 1-inch (2.5-cm) air vents into the top layer of dough.

Bake for 10 to 12 minutes, or until the edges are golden. If you wish, broil for 1 minute at the end to give the top crust more color before serving.

Easy Baked Strawberry Cobbler

SERVINGS: 10
ESTIMATED CALORIES:
182 per serving

I'm a sucker for fresh and fruity cobblers, and this one takes first place! My strawberry cobbler is always a favorite among vegans and non-vegans alike! The heavenly aroma of juicy berries and buttery sweet crumble baking in the oven will draw everyone in. Mouths will water while everybody waits, not so patiently, for this craveable cobbler to finish. While this dish tastes indulgent and comforting, it is actually made with some good-for-you ingredients.

Nonstick spray, for dish

6 cups (864 g) fresh or frozen strawberries

½ cup (120 ml) melted coconut oil or vegan butter

⅓ cup (40 g) coconut sugar or cane sugar

1 tbsp (15 ml) unsweetened almond milk

1 tsp vanilla extract

1 tsp baking powder

½ tsp ground cinnamon

¼ tsp salt

1 cup (125 g) regular or gluten-free all-purpose flour (for gluten-free, I like King Arthur Gluten Free Measure for Measure)

Preheat the oven to 350°F (175°C). Spray a 9 x 11-inch (23 x 28-cm) casserole dish or 11- to 12-inch (28- to 30-cm) round baking dish with nonstick spray.

Pour the strawberries into the prepared baking dish.

In a medium-sized bowl, use a fork or whisk to mix together the melted coconut oil, sugar, almond milk, vanilla, baking powder, cinnamon and salt. Then, add the flour until a thick, biscuitlike dough forms. Use your hands to evenly crumble the dough over the berries.

Bake for 30 to 40 minutes, or until the cobbler topping is golden brown and cooked through. The berries should be tender and juicy. Remove from the oven and allow the cobbler to cool for about 5 minutes before serving warm from the dish.

Papa Bear's Pumpkin Pie

One of my dad's favorite things to enjoy over the holiday season is my famous pumpkin pie! He's probably the least vegan person that I know, and even he loves this recipe. I've included my easy classic piecrust and Pop's favorite graham cracker piecrust for you to choose from. No matter how you slice it, this pie is going to steal the show!

SERVINGS: 12
ESTIMATED CALORIES: 229 per serving

CLASSIC PIECRUST

¾ cup (180 ml) unsweetened almond milk

½ cup (120 ml) melted vegan butter or coconut oil

1 tbsp (15 ml) pure maple syrup

1½ tsp (7 g) baking powder

2 cups (250 g) regular or gluten-free all-purpose flour (for gluten-free, I like King Arthur Gluten Free Measure for Measure), plus more for dusting

GRAHAM CRACKER PIECRUST (OPTIONAL; REDUCES EACH SERVING BY 27 CALORIES)

12 vegan graham crackers, crushed

½ cup (120 ml) melted vegan butter or coconut oil

¼ cup (50 g) coconut or cane sugar

PUMPKIN PIE FILLING

2½ cups (600 ml) canned pure pumpkin puree

1 cup (240 ml) canned full-fat coconut milk

⅓ cup (31 g) coconut sugar

¼ cup (50 g) monk fruit sweetener with erythritol

1 tsp vanilla extract

1 tsp ground cinnamon

½ tsp ground nutmeg

½ tsp ground cloves

½ tsp ground ginger

3 tbsp (24 g) cornstarch

¼ tsp salt

Preheat the oven to 350°F (175°C).

To prepare the classic piecrust: In a medium-sized bowl, use a fork or whisk to mix together the almond milk, melted vegan butter, maple syrup and baking powder. Then, add the flour and mix until a dough forms.

Roll out the dough on a floured surface to form a 10- to 12-inch (25- to 30-cm) circle, as appropriate for your pie dish. Drape the crust into a pie dish, then use your fingers to press the dough into the dish. Trim the edges or leave it looking rustic. Do not prebake this crust.

To prepare the graham cracker piecrust (if using): In a medium-sized bowl, mix together the crushed graham crackers, melted vegan butter and sugar. Then, press the mixture evenly into a pie dish and bake for about 10 minutes. Remove the crust from the oven, allow to cool and proceed.

Prepare the pumpkin pie filling: In a large bowl, use a whisk to mix together the pumpkin puree, coconut milk, coconut sugar, monk fruit sweetener, vanilla, cinnamon, nutmeg, cloves, ginger, cornstarch and salt. Pour over your choice of piecrust and bake for about 50 minutes, or until it begins to crack on top.

Remove the pie from the oven, let cool, then refrigerate it for about 2 hours (or preferably overnight) before serving it straight from the pie dish. This recipe tastes delicious with a little coconut whipped cream or confectioners' sugar on top.

8-Ingredient Cherry Pie Oatmeal

SERVINGS: 10

ESTIMATED CALORIES:
164 per serving
(without frosting)

Imagine merging the smell and taste of warm baked oatmeal with a slice of gooey cherry pie. Two of my favorite comfort foods join forces here to create a wholesome, delicious dessert that will make you feel right at home. Baked oatmeal is nutritious, comforting and super filling. If you love cherry pie but are searching for a healthier, vegan and optionally gluten-free version that is quick and easy, and tastes indulgent, this recipe is for you! It makes a great make-ahead breakfast or weeknight dessert.

CHERRY PIE OATMEAL BAKE

Nonstick spray, for dish

1 cup (240 ml) unsweetened almond milk

¾ cup (150 g) coconut sugar, cane sugar or pure maple syrup

¼ cup (60 ml) melted vegan butter

1 tsp baking powder

1 tsp vanilla extract

½ tsp ground cinnamon

2 cups (180 g) quick oats (certified gluten-free, if needed)

2 cups (308 g) diced frozen cherries

VEGAN CREAM CHEESE FROSTING (OPTIONAL; ADDS 75 CALORIES PER SERVING)

2 oz (57 g) vegan cream cheese

2 tbsp (28 g) softened vegan butter

¾ cup (90 g) confectioners' sugar

Prepare the cherry pie oatmeal bake: Preheat the oven to 375°F (190°C). Spray a 9 x 11–inch (23 x 28–cm) casserole dish with nonstick spray.

In a large bowl, use a fork to mix together the almond milk, coconut sugar, melted vegan butter, baking powder, vanilla and cinnamon. Then, add the quick oats and mix. Fold in the cherries and pour the batter into the prepared casserole dish.

Bake for 40 minutes. The oatmeal bake should be golden brown around the edges and the cherries should be bubbling.

Meanwhile, prepare the cream cheese frosting: In a medium-sized bowl, mix together the vegan cream cheese, softened vegan butter and confectioners' sugar.

Remove the oatmeal bake from the oven and allow to cool before drizzling with the frosting. Enjoy as a comforting dessert or breakfast.

5-Ingredient Healthy Oatmeal Apple Crisp

SERVINGS: 8
ESTIMATED CALORIES: 165 per serving

This wholesome crisp is absolutely divine! Juicy apples are baked to perfection, and the sweet and cinnamon-spiced topping is golden, buttery and delicious. This is a healthy dessert that provides all the comforting indulgent flavors of a traditional apple crisp with a fraction of the calories and sugar. Serve it with your favorite oat milk ice cream, yogurt, or top it with coconut whipped cream for a nutritious, filling and guilt-free vegan dessert that everyone will love! I bet you already have all the ingredients you need in your pantry!

Nonstick spray, for dish

4 medium-sized Honeycrisp apples, sliced in half and then cut into thin slices

¼ cup (60 ml) melted coconut oil or vegan butter

¼ cup (50 g) cane or coconut sugar

½ tsp ground cinnamon

1 cup (90 g) quick oats (certified gluten-free, if needed)

Preheat the oven to 425°F (220°C). Spray a 9- to 10-inch (23- to 25-cm) baking dish with nonstick spray.

Arrange the sliced apples in the prepared baking dish.

In a small bowl, mix together the melted coconut oil, sugar, cinnamon and quick oats. Sprinkle the oat mixture over the apples. Bake for 20 to 25 minutes, until the oats are golden. If desired, broil for 1 to 2 minutes at the end to brown the top.

Serve warm for breakfast or dessert. This stores well in the fridge and can be reheated in the microwave.

Craving Peach Cobbler

SERVINGS: 8
ESTIMATED CALORIES:
137 per serving

While I was growing up, my family would take a road trip to South Carolina to see my stepdad's family for the holidays. My stepdad has a huge family and his sister would make the most incredible peach cobbler. Okay, it wasn't really a cobbler. We called it a "dump cake." It was essentially canned peach pie filling with a box of cake mix dumped on top. That dump cake inspired this crowd-pleasing cobbler that everyone in my family now loves. Instead of peach pie filling, I use sliced peaches and allow their natural sweetness to shine through when baked. Instead of loads of butter, I use the healthier coconut oil. Instead of cake mix, I go with oats and flour. Ya'll, I can't lie—it's as outstanding as my aunt's cobbler . . . and a whole lot healthier.

Nonstick spray, for dish

4 cups (616 g) sliced fresh or frozen peaches

½ cup (100 g) coconut sugar or light brown sugar

⅓ cup (80 ml) unsweetened applesauce

¼ cup (60 ml) melted vegan butter or coconut oil

1 tsp vanilla extract

1 tsp ground cinnamon

¼ tsp salt

1 cup (90 g) quick oats (certified gluten-free, if needed)

¼ cup (31 g) oat flour (certified gluten-free, if needed) or regular or gluten-free all-purpose flour (for gluten-free, I like King Arthur Gluten Free Measure for Measure)

Preheat the oven to 350°F (175°C). Spray a 9 x 11–inch (23 x 28–cm) casserole dish with nonstick spray.

Arrange the peaches in the prepared casserole dish. In a medium-sized bowl, mix together the sugar, applesauce, melted vegan butter, vanilla, cinnamon and salt. Then, mix in the oats and oat flour. Pour the oat crumble over the peaches.

Bake for 35 to 40 minutes, or until the peaches are tender and the crumble is crisp and golden brown. Allow the dish to cool for about 5 minutes, then serve warm. This tastes amazing topped with coconut milk whipped cream or a scoop of oat milk ice cream.

Southern-Style Sweet Potato Oatmeal Streusel

SERVINGS: 8
ESTIMATED CALORIES:
261 per serving

If you've never had sweet potato streusel, this recipe might change your life. Imagine a sweet potato casserole, but so much better. Creamy sweet potatoes are topped with a homemade streusel that's vegan, healthy and unbelievably yummy. It's made with coconut sugar, melted vegan butter (or coconut oil) and oats. You know how it's always hard to not go for seconds at the Thanksgiving table? Well, good luck not wanting seconds—or thirds—of this crazy-good oatmeal streusel! It makes for a deliciously rich and hearty dessert. I've even served this for breakfast!

Nonstick spray, for dish

6 cups (804 g) peeled and diced sweet potatoes (about 3 large sweet potatoes)

¾ cup (68 g) quick oats (certified gluten-free, if needed)

½ cup (50 g) coconut sugar or light brown sugar, divided

¼ cup (60 ml) melted vegan butter or coconut oil

2 tbsp (16 g) oat flour (certified gluten-free if needed), or regular or gluten-free all-purpose flour (for gluten-free, I like King Arthur Gluten Free Measure for Measure)

2 tbsp (14 g) crushed pecans

2 tsp (5 g) ground cinnamon, divided

1 cup (240 ml) unsweetened almond milk

2 tbsp (28 g) softened vegan butter or coconut oil

1 tsp vanilla extract

Preheat the oven to 350°F (175°C). Spray an 8 x 8–inch (20 x 20–cm) or 9 x 11–inch (23 x 28–cm) casserole dish with nonstick spray.

Bring a large pot of water to a boil. Once boiling, add the sweet potatoes and lower the heat to a simmer. Simmer, uncovered, until the potatoes are soft and tender, about 25 minutes.

While the potatoes cook, prepare the oatmeal crumble: In a medium-sized bowl, use a fork to mix together the quick oats, ¼ cup (30 g) of the sugar, melted vegan butter, oat flour, crushed pecans and 1 teaspoon of the cinnamon. Set aside.

Once the potatoes are done, drain and place them in a large bowl. Add the almond milk, softened vegan butter, remaining ¼ cup (30 g) of sugar, remaining teaspoon of cinnamon and vanilla. Use a handheld immersion blender to blend.

Pour the blended sweet potatoes evenly into the prepared dish. Evenly distribute the oatmeal streusel over the sweet potatoes.

Bake for 35 to 40 minutes, or until the oatmeal crumble is golden brown. Remove from the oven and allow to cool for 5 to 10 minutes, then serve immediately with a side of oat milk ice cream.

QUICK, SATISFYING BREADS, BISCUITS AND BITES

Carb lovers, prepare to have your hankering satisfied!

There's nothing better than the smell of homemade bread circulating through your home. In the past, you may have been intimated by homemade breads or biscuits—but these recipes are so easy that anyone can make them! Every sweet and savory recipe within this chapter is vegan, can be made gluten-free and is certain to satisfy your carb craving.

We kick things off with my Must-Try Banana Bread (page 80). This buttery, tender vegan banana bread is made with wholesome and healthy oats, maple syrup, ripe bananas and one bowl. I'm going to be honest, this is perhaps one of the best-tasting banana breads you'll ever have and will quickly become a favorite among your family and friends (as it has mine). Speaking of crowd-pleasing recipes, my Super-Moist Blackberry Lemon Loaf (page 92) drizzled with vegan cream cheese frosting is going to knock everyone's vegan and non-vegan socks off! We move on to savory bites, such as Salted Soft Baked Pretzel Bites (page 83), which are surprisingly easy and dangerously delicious! Don't even get me started on my famous Unbelievable Vegan Biscuits (page 84) that are beloved by my whole family of non-vegans and incredibly versatile! And you haven't lived until you try dipping a piece of Vegan Pull-Apart Cheesy Bread (page 103) into marinara sauce. Whether you're in the mood for a sweet or savory indulgence, this chapter has everything you need to make your low-calorie vegan bread dreams come true.

Must-Try Banana Bread

One soft slice of this delicious and super-moist banana bread will explain why it's a must-try recipe! This is one of my most popular recipes and for good reason! Banana bread is one of those baked goods that tugs on my heartstrings, and you're going to fall in love with this one. This incredible vegan version is buttery, thick and perfectly sweet, thanks to three overripe bananas and a bit of maple syrup. This is an indulgent tasting and wholesome banana bread that no one will be able to get enough of! Trust me when I say, it will become a go-to for you and your family. PS: Definitely lick the batter from the bowl on this one—it's delicious!

SERVINGS: 12
ESTIMATED CALORIES: 174 per serving

Nonstick spray, for pan

3 medium-sized overripe bananas, mashed

1 cup (240 ml) unsweetened almond milk

¾ cup (180 ml) pure maple syrup

¼ cup (60 ml) melted vegan butter

1 tsp vanilla extract

1 tsp ground cinnamon

1 tsp baking soda

2 tsp (9 g) baking powder

1 cup (90 g) quick oats (certified gluten-free, if needed)

1½ cups (188 g) regular or gluten-free all-purpose flour (for gluten-free, I like King Arthur Gluten Free Measure for Measure)

Preheat the oven to 375°F (190°C). Spray a 9 x 5–inch (23 x 13–cm) loaf pan with nonstick spray.

In a medium-sized bowl, mix together the bananas, almond milk, maple syrup, melted vegan butter, vanilla, cinnamon, baking soda and baking powder. Then, mix in the quick oats and flour just until smooth.

Pour the batter into the prepared loaf pan. (Don't forget to lick the spoon!) Bake the bread for 40 to 50 minutes, or until golden brown on top. Check it with a toothpick inserted into the center—you'll know it's done when the toothpick comes out clean.

Remove from the loaf pan and serve warm on its own, or spread with a little softened vegan butter and drizzle with maple syrup. This bread keeps well on the countertop wrapped in plastic for 3 to 5 days.

Salted Soft Baked Pretzel Bites

MAKES
about 80 bites
ESTIMATED CALORIES:
17 per bite

When I was a kid and my mom would take me to the mall, I'd beg her to take me to get pretzel bites. There was something about those little salty bites of boiled, baked and buttery pretzels that made the whole experience better. Now, I can enjoy one of my favorite salty snacks right at home—no need to wait to go to the mall or a sporting event to enjoy this classic treat! These vegan pretzel bites are so satisfying and they smell almost as amazing as they taste! Plus, they're easy to make with just a few simple ingredients. Put a plate of these on your table and watch them disappear before your eyes.

1 cup (240 ml) warm water

2 tbsp (30 ml) melted vegan butter

1 tbsp (15 ml) pure maple syrup

1 tbsp (12 g) active dry yeast

2½ cups (312 g) regular or gluten-free all-purpose flour (for gluten-free, I like King Arthur Gluten Free Measure for Measure), plus more for dusting

2 tbsp (28 g) baking soda

Olive oil spray

1 tbsp (18 g) sea salt

Preheat the oven to 400°F (200°C). Line a baking sheet with parchment paper.

In a large bowl, mix the warm water with the melted vegan butter and maple syrup. Sprinkle the yeast on top of the mixture and stir a few times. Let the mixture sit for 5 to 10 minutes, or until the yeast begins to fizzle and bloom.

Mix in the flour, using your hands to form the dough into a mound in the bowl. Cover the bowl with a clean kitchen towel and allow it to rise for 1 hour. My trick to letting the dough rise faster is to set the bowl on top of a preheated oven. You will know it has risen when the dough has doubled in size.

After the dough rises, separate it into eight pieces and, on a floured surface, use your hands to roll each into an 8- to 10-inch (20- to 25-cm) strip. Slice the strips of dough into about ten pieces.

Make a baking soda bath: In a large pot, bring 6 cups (1.4 L) of water to a slow boil. Then, lower the heat to a low boil and add the baking soda. The baking soda will fizzle. Working in batches, drop about ten pieces of the pretzel dough into the baking soda water and use a large slotted spoon to remove each piece within about 5 seconds.

Place the boiled dough on the prepared baking sheet, spacing them about 1 inch (2.5 cm) apart, and bake for 20 minutes, or until the pretzel bites are golden brown on the outside and completely baked on the inside. Repeat this process until all the dough is used.

Remove the bites from the oven, then spray them with the olive oil spray and sprinkle the sea salt on top. Serve them on their own or dipped in vegan cheese sauce, mustard or any of your other favorite pretzel dips.

Unbelievable Vegan Biscuits—5 Ways

MAKES 12 biscuits
ESTIMATED CALORIES: 144 per plain biscuit

Buttery, golden and crisp on the outside, pillowy soft and fluffy on the inside. I'm a southern girl, and I grew up on biscuits. Traditional biscuits can be time consuming to make, and they definitely aren't vegan! These drop biscuits require no kneading, folding or cutting. They're vegan, can be made gluten-free and are super versatile. Oh, and they're ready in about 15 minutes! Enjoy them as plain butter biscuits and—y'all, I'm telling you—you won't believe how good they are! Spread them with a little vegan butter and jam for a classic southern-style biscuit.

Let's talk about variations: Speaking of the South, we have a fast-food place down here that used to serve something called "Bo-Berry" biscuits! That's right—a biscuit loaded with juicy blueberries, topped with icing. Or try these drizzled with maple butter for a breakfast or dessert biscuit that will please every palate. In the mood for a savory biscuit? Ever been to Red Lobster? That's right—you can turn these into "Cheddar Bay" biscuits and brush them with melted vegan butter. Recreate any of these famous biscuits at home with a few added ingredients and no added time. And, for the everything bagel lovers of the universe, top these biscuits with everything bagel seasoning and smear them with your favorite vegan cream cheese.

6-INGREDIENT DROP BISCUITS

¾ cup (180 ml) unsweetened almond milk

½ cup (120 ml) melted vegan butter

1 tbsp (15 ml) pure maple syrup

1½ tsp (7 g) baking powder

¼ tsp salt

2 cups (250 g) regular or gluten-free all-purpose flour (for gluten-free, I like King Arthur Gluten Free Measure for Measure)

"BO-BERRY" BISCUITS (ADD 25 CALORIES PER BISCUIT)

2 tsp (10 ml) vanilla extract, divided

1 cup (148 g) frozen wild blueberries or strawberries

½ cup (60 g) confectioners' sugar

1 tbsp (15 ml) unsweetened almond milk

Prepare the biscuit dough: Preheat the oven to 400°F (200°C). Line a baking sheet with parchment paper.

In a large bowl, use a fork to mix together the almond milk, melted vegan butter, maple syrup, baking powder and salt. If making "Bo-Berry" biscuits, add 1 teaspoon of the vanilla to your batter. Then, mix in the flour just until combined. Be careful not to overmix, or else the biscuits will be dense.

For "Bo-Berry" biscuits, fold the blueberries into the 6-ingredient dough. For "Cheddar Bay" biscuits, fold the Cheddar cheese shreds, garlic powder and parsley into the 6-ingredient dough.

Use a heaping tablespoon to scoop out 12 biscuits and drop them directly onto the prepared baking sheet, spacing them about 1½ inches (4 cm) apart.

For everything bagel biscuits, sprinkle the seasoning on top of the 6-ingredient-dough biscuits before baking. For plain butter or maple butter biscuits, proceed to next the step.

Bake for about 15 minutes, or until lightly golden on top. If desired, broil at the end for about 1 minute to give the biscuits more color. Remove from the oven.

(continued)

Maple Butter Biscuits

6-Ingredient Drop Biscuits

Bo-Berry Biscuits

Bo-Berry Biscuits with Strawberries

"Cheddar Bay" Biscuits

Everything Bagel Biscuits

"CHEDDAR BAY" BISCUITS
(ADD 41 CALORIES PER BISCUIT)

1 cup (113 g) vegan Cheddar cheese shreds

1 tsp garlic powder

1 tbsp (4 g) chopped fresh parsley

1 tbsp (15 ml) melted vegan butter

EVERYTHING BAGEL BISCUITS
(ADD 5 CALORIES PER BISCUIT)

¼ cup (40 g) everything bagel seasoning, store-bought or homemade (page 109)

MAPLE BUTTER BISCUITS
(ADD 25 CALORIES PER BISCUIT)

2 tbsp (30 ml) pure maple syrup

2 tbsp (30 ml) melted vegan butter

For maple butter biscuits, just before serving, mix together the maple syrup and melted vegan butter. Allow the biscuits to cool for a couple of minutes, then brush or drizzle the warm biscuits with the maple butter.

If making "Bo-Berry" biscuits, prepare the icing: In a small bowl, use a whisk to mix together the confectioners' sugar, almond milk and the remaining teaspoon of vanilla. Allow the biscuits to cool for 2 minutes, then drizzle them with the icing.

If making "Cheddar Bay" biscuits, allow them to cool and then brush them with the melted vegan butter.

Serve the plain or everything seasoned biscuits with vegan butter, cream cheese or jam. You may also slice them in half to use as breakfast sandwich buns.

Georgia Gal's Blueberry Cornbread

SERVINGS: 12
ESTIMATED CALORIES: 150 per serving

Y'all know I'm a Georgia gal! And, you also probably know by now that I am a certified bread lover! Whenever Thanksgiving comes around, I'm not drawn to the meat or savory sides—I'm a cornbread girl through and through! There's nothing like a thick, crumbly slice of homemade cornbread with a little vegan butter. Thanks to the coconut milk in this cornbread, you won't miss the eggs and dairy found in a traditional cornbread. Coconut milk isn't the only wholesome ingredient in this loaf—delicious blueberries and healthy flaxseed meal make this loaf as good for you as it is craveably delicious!

Nonstick spray, for pan

2 tbsp (20 g) flaxseed meal

¼ cup (60 ml) warm water

1 (13.5-oz [400-ml]) can full-fat coconut milk

4 tbsp (60 ml) melted vegan butter

2 tbsp (30 ml) maple syrup

2 tsp (9 g) baking powder

½ tsp salt

1 cup (125 g) regular or gluten-free all-purpose flour (for gluten-free, I like King Arthur Gluten Free Measure for Measure)

1 cup (125 g) cornmeal

1 cup (88 g) frozen wild blueberries

Vegan butter or agave nectar, for serving

Preheat the oven to 400°F (200°C). Spray a 9 x 5–inch (23 x 13–cm) loaf pan with nonstick spray.

In a small bowl, mix the flaxseed meal with the warm water. Set aside for 2 minutes, or until a gel forms, to make flax eggs.

In a medium-size bowl, mix together the flax eggs, coconut milk, melted vegan butter, maple syrup, baking powder and salt. Then, mix in the flour and cornmeal until combined. Fold in the frozen blueberries and pour the batter into the prepared loaf pan.

Bake for 30 to 35 minutes, or until the edges of the cornbread are golden. Test the center with a toothpick; if it doesn't come out clean, it isn't done. Continue to bake until the cornbread is completely baked through in the center. If it begins to brown too much on the top, cover the pan loosely with foil to protect it from the heat.

Remove the loaf from the oven and allow it to cool before serving with vegan butter or drizzled with agave nectar.

Sugary Lemon Sweet Rolls

MAKES 20 rolls
ESTIMATED CALORIES:
143 per serving
(without frosting)

Lemon, butter, sugar, oh my! Three of life's greatest pleasures baked into a batch of golden sweet rolls. These sugary, sticky rolls are as beautiful to look at as they are to eat. The bright citrusy flavor will make your mouth water. You will completely forget that these are lighter and vegan! This recipe begins with a soft and buttery biscuit-style sweet roll dough, brightened up with lemon juice. We fill it with vegan butter and sugar . . . yum! Bake and serve for breakfast, brunch or dessert. I find these rolls are great on their own, but they taste even more amazing with my vegan cream cheese frosting.

DOUGH

½ cup (120 ml) unsweetened almond milk

½ cup (120 ml) melted vegan butter

½ cup (120 ml) fresh lemon juice

2 tbsp (30 ml) pure maple syrup

1½ tsp (7 g) baking powder

3 cups (375 g) regular or gluten-free all-purpose flour (for gluten-free, I like King Arthur Gluten Free Measure for Measure), plus more for dusting

FILLING

¼ cup (57 g) softened vegan butter

¼ cup (50 g) cane sugar

VEGAN CREAM CHEESE FROSTING (OPTIONAL; ADDS 38 CALORIES PER SERVING)

¾ cup (90 g) confectioners' sugar

2 tbsp (28 g) softened vegan butter

2 oz (57 g) softened vegan cream cheese

Preheat the oven to 375°F (190°C).

Prepare the dough: In a large bowl, use a fork or whisk to mix together the almond milk, melted vegan butter, lemon juice, maple syrup and baking powder. Then, add the flour and mix until a thick dough forms.

Place the dough on a well-floured surface and roll it out into a ¼-inch (6-mm)-thick slab. Add the filling: Spread with softened vegan butter and sprinkle evenly with the cane sugar. Roll it up into a log and slice into about 20 pinwheels, each about 1 inch (2.5 cm) thick and 1½ inches (4 cm) wide. Place them in a single layer in a 10- to 12-inch (25- to 30-cm) round baking dish so that they are all touching.

Bake for about 25 minutes, or until lightly golden. If desired, broil for 1 minute at the end to give them more color.

While the rolls bake, prepare the cream cheese frosting (if using): In a medium-sized bowl, use a whisk or electric hand mixer to mix together the confectioners' sugar, softened vegan butter and softened vegan cream cheese until smooth. Spoon the frosting over the warm rolls after you've allowed them to cool for about 5 minutes.

Super-Moist Blackberry Lemon Loaf

SERVINGS: 12

ESTIMATED CALORIES:
190 per serving
(without frosting)

This is one of my most popular recipes with vegans and non-vegans alike—a "berry yummy," better-for-you spin on lemon cake. It's perfectly sweet, lemony and beyond delicious. The juicy blackberries make the perfect addition to this tender lemon loaf cake. No blackberries? No problem—use any berry (calories may vary) in this delectable loaf. You have the option to top the baked loaf with my vegan cream cheese frosting that tastes utterly amazing. Even without frosting, it's absolutely mouthwatering! This vegan sweet treat is perfect for any occasion and will be popular among your friends and family.

Note: Change it up by swapping the blackberries for any of your favorite berries in this recipe (calories vary) or enjoy this super-moist loaf as a classic lemon cake by leaving out the berries completely.

SUPER-MOIST BLACKBERRY LEMON LOAF

Nonstick spray, for pan

1 cup (240 ml) unsweetened almond milk

1 cup (200 g) cane sugar (see Tips)

½ cup (120 ml) fresh lemon juice

¼ cup (60 ml) melted vegan butter

1 tsp vanilla extract

1½ tsp (7 g) baking powder

1 tsp baking soda

2¼ cups (281 g) regular or gluten-free all-purpose flour (for gluten-free, I like King Arthur Gluten Free Measure for Measure)

2 cups (246 g) fresh blackberries or any other berries

VEGAN CREAM CHEESE FROSTING (OPTIONAL; ADDS 43 CALORIES PER SERVING)

¾ cup (90 g) confectioners' sugar

2 tbsp (28 g) softened vegan butter

2 oz (57 g) vegan cream cheese

Prepare the loaf: Preheat the oven to 375°F (190°C). Spray a 9 x 5–inch (23 x 13–cm) metal loaf pan with nonstick spray.

In a large bowl, using a fork or whisk, mix together the almond milk, cane sugar, lemon juice, melted vegan butter and vanilla. Next, add the baking powder and baking soda and then mix. Then, quickly add the flour and mix until combined. Fold in the blackberries.

Pour the batter into the prepared loaf pan and bake for 40 to 45 minutes, or until golden on the edges. Test for doneness by sticking a toothpick into the center; when it comes out clean, the loaf is done.

While the loaf bakes, prepare the cream cheese frosting (if using). In a medium-sized bowl, use an electric hand mixer to mix the confectioners' sugar, softened vegan butter and vegan cream cheese.

Spread the frosting over the warm loaf and serve immediately.

This stores well for up to 3 days in an airtight container at room temperature.

TIPS: Use ¼ cup (50 g) of cane sugar plus 4 teaspoons (10 g) of pure powdered stevia in place of the cup of cane sugar, for a reduced-sugar and low-cal swap! The result is 140 calories per unfrosted slice. For lemon lovers: This loaf has a wonderfully light lemon flavor; to make it even more lemony, you may add 1 teaspoon of lemon extract.

One-Bowl Chocolate–Coconut Milk Loaf

SERVINGS: 12
ESTIMATED CALORIES:
183 per serving

Chocolate lovers, I have a better-for-you version of the chocolate cake you love! Don't let the words "better-for-you" deceive you—it tastes even more chocolaty, tender and delicious than the chocolate cakes you're used to, almost like a brownie and a cake baked into one scrumptious loaf! My secret weapons are coconut milk and maple syrup, rather than milk and table sugar. Coconut milk has healthy fats that are great for your body and make baked goods super moist. It's very mild, so you won't notice any coconut flavor—just the sweetened cocoa taste you desire. This recipe uses one bowl, 5 minutes of prep time and 40 to bake—and you're going to love it down to the last chocolaty slice.

Nonstick spray, for pan

1 (13.5-oz [400-ml]) can full-fat coconut milk

¾ cup (180 ml) pure maple syrup

2 tsp (10 ml) vanilla extract

1 tsp baking powder

1 tsp baking soda

¼ cup (22 g) unsweetened cocoa powder

2 cups (250 g) regular or gluten-free all-purpose flour (for gluten-free, I like King Arthur Gluten Free Measure for Measure)

3 tbsp (32 g) vegan chocolate chips (optional; adds 15 calories per serving)

Preheat the oven to 375°F (190°C). Spray a 9 x 5–inch (23 x 13–cm) loaf pan with nonstick spray.

In a large bowl, use a fork or whisk to mix together the coconut milk, maple syrup, vanilla, baking powder, baking soda and cocoa powder. Then, add the flour and mix until a batter forms. It's your choice whether to fold in the chocolate chips, sprinkle them on top once the batter is in the pan or omit them.

Pour the batter into the prepared loaf pan, sprinkling with the chocolate chips, if desired, and bake for 40 to 45 minutes, or until completely risen through the middle. You can check for doneness by sticking a toothpick into the center to see if it comes out clean.

Remove the loaf from the pan and serve on a platter. I love a slice of this on its own, but you can spread it with nut butter or softened vegan butter for an even more indulgent treat.

This loaf can be stored wrapped in plastic on the counter for 3 to 5 days.

Apple-Cinnamon Soft Baked Biscuits

MAKES 12 biscuits

ESTIMATED CALORIES:
121 per biscuit
(without icing)

These warm freshly baked biscuits are crisp on the outside, soft on the inside and flavored with subtle notes of spiced and sweet apples. Apple cinnamon is a flavor combination that everyone loves. The comforting flavors taste like home. These biscuits bring a ton of warmth to the plate. This recipe is the perfect low-cal vegan breakfast, brunch or dessert because it's sweetened with monk fruit, a hint of vanilla and that wonderfully homey flavor of apple and cinnamon. It's your choice whether to drizzle with the almond milk icing or enjoy as is for a lower-calorie option. No matter which you choose, you're going to love sinking your teeth into each cinnamon-spiced bite.

BISCUITS

¾ cup (180 ml) unsweetened almond milk

⅓ cup (80 ml) melted vegan butter

⅓ cup (80 ml) unsweetened applesauce

2 tbsp (30 g) monk fruit sweetener with erythritol or cane or coconut sugar

1½ tsp (7 g) baking powder

1 tsp ground cinnamon

1 tsp vanilla extract

2 cups (250 g) regular or gluten-free all-purpose flour (for gluten-free, I like King Arthur Gluten Free Measure for Measure)

ALMOND MILK ICING (OPTIONAL; ADDS 20 CALORIES PER BISCUIT)

½ cup (60 g) confectioners' sugar

1 tbsp (15 ml) unsweetened almond milk

1 tsp vanilla extract

Prepare the biscuits: Preheat the oven to 400°F (200°C). Line a baking sheet with parchment paper.

In a large bowl, use a fork or whisk to mix together the almond milk, melted vegan butter, applesauce, monk fruit sweetener, baking powder, cinnamon and vanilla. Then, add the flour and mix just until a fluffy dough forms.

Use a tablespoon to drop the dough onto the prepared baking sheet, spacing the mounds about 2 inches (5 cm) apart. This recipe makes about 12 biscuits. Bake for 12 to 15 minutes, or until the tops are lightly golden. If desired, broil for 1 minute at the end to give the biscuits more color.

While the biscuits bake, prepare the almond milk icing (if using): In a medium-sized bowl, use an electric hand mixer to mix the confectioners' sugar, almond milk and vanilla.

Remove the biscuits from the oven and allow them to cool for about 2 minutes, then drizzle with the icing (if using). Serve warm.

If you loved these, be sure to check out the cookie chapter of this book, and feast your eyes and taste buds on my delicious Apple Pie–Cinnamon Sugar Cookies (page 17).

Sweet Orange Rolls

At my family gatherings, there's always a basket of freshly baked bread or rolls on the table. My bonus mom serves the most delicious spreads and never holds back on the carbs. There's nothing better than the smell and taste of homemade bread, fresh from the oven. Everyone in your home will want to dive right into this golden and glazed batch of freshly baked goodness. The olive oil makes each bite of bread wonderfully moist and dense, while the orange juice and maple syrup bring a light sweetness. These are perfect for your breakfast or brunch table and even more perfect to slice in half and use as mini sandwich rolls.

MAKES 12 rolls

ESTIMATED CALORIES: 156 per roll

Nonstick spray, for dish

½ cup (120 ml) olive oil or melted vegan butter

½ cup (120 ml) unsweetened almond milk

⅓ cup (80 ml) fresh orange juice

¼ cup (60 ml) pure maple syrup

1½ tsp (7 g) baking powder

2 cups (250 g) regular or gluten free all-purpose flour (for gluten-free, I like King Arthur Gluten Free Measure for Measure)

Zest of 1 small orange (optional)

Preheat the oven to 400°F (200°C). Spray a 9 x 11–inch (23 x 28–cm) baking dish or casserole dish with nonstick spray.

In a large bowl, mix together the olive oil, almond milk, orange juice, maple syrup and baking powder. Then, add the flour and mix just until combined. Be careful not to overmix the bread dough or else it will become too dense.

Evenly distribute the dough in the prepared dish. Bake for about 25 minutes, or until golden around the edges. To give it a bit more color, broil for 1 minute at the end. You can also top them with a little orange zest, if you'd like.

These rolls are perfectly sweet and moist and taste amazing drizzled with a little agave nectar or maple syrup. Serve warm with your favorite breakfast pairings or slice in half to use as sandwich buns.

Cinnamon-Spiced Sweet Potato Bread

SERVINGS: 12
ESTIMATED CALORIES: 168 per serving

My mom has food nicknames for my brother and me. Because I'm so short, my nickname is "Peanut." My brother's is "Sweet Potato," because as a baby he would gobble up sweet potatoes! This healthy and delicious bread is inspired by my sweet little brother. Whether enjoying a slice buttered with breakfast, drizzled with maple syrup for dessert or as a side to your favorite homestyle dish—there's always room at your table for this dense and moist sweet potato bread. It's egg and dairy-free, super easy and surprisingly wholesome. Are you a pumpkin bread lover? You can swap out the sweet potato puree for pure pumpkin puree in this recipe. PS: "Pumpkin" was one of my other nicknames while growing up. Now you see why I love food so much!

Nonstick spray, for pan

1 cup (240 g) cooked and mashed sweet potato or pumpkin puree

1 cup (240 ml) unsweetened almond milk

½ cup (120 ml) pure maple syrup

¼ cup (60 ml) melted vegan butter or coconut oil

1 tsp vanilla extract

1 tbsp (15 ml) cider vinegar

1½ tsp (7 g) baking powder

1 tsp baking soda

1 tsp ground cinnamon

¼ tsp salt

¼ tsp ground nutmeg (optional)

¼ tsp ground ginger (optional)

⅛ tsp ground cloves (optional)

2¼ cups (281 g) oat flour (certified gluten-free, if needed; see Tip)

½ cup (45 g) quick oats (certified gluten-free, if needed; see Tip)

Preheat the oven to 375°F (190°C). Spray a 9 x 5–inch (23 x 13–cm) loaf pan with nonstick spray.

In a large bowl, mix together the sweet potato, almond milk, maple syrup, melted vegan butter, vanilla, cider vinegar, baking powder, baking soda, cinnamon and salt. Add the nutmeg, ginger and cloves, if desired. Mix in the oat flour and quick oats.

Pour the batter into the prepared loaf pan. Bake for 40 to 45 minutes, or until the loaf is completely risen and you can stick a toothpick into the center and it comes out clean.

Remove the bread from the pan and serve sliced and spread with a little softened vegan butter or drizzled with maple syrup. This bread stores well wrapped in plastic on the countertop for up to 5 days.

TIP: No oats? No problem! You may use 2 cups (250 g) regular or gluten-free all-purpose flour in place of the oat flour and quick oats. This lowers the calorie count by 15 calories per slice.

Vegan Pull-Apart Cheesy Bread

SERVINGS: 16
ESTIMATED CALORIES:
149 per serving
with yeast dough
/ 123 per serving
with no-yeast
dough

When I was a kid, I would look forward to "Pizza Fridays." It wasn't about the pizza for me—when we were ordering in, my bonus mom always knew to throw in an order of cheesy bread for me. Cheesy pull-apart bread is the epitome of everything delicious in this world. And just because you're vegan doesn't mean you have to miss out on a batch of fluffy and buttery dough topped with melted vegan mozzarella! Enjoy the cheesy bread sticks alone or dunk them into your favorite homemade (page 106) or store-bought marinara sauce. Not only will you be reminded of the cheesy bread in the pizza delivery box, but you'll prefer this vegan version!

I've included two options for the dough: The first is my classic yeast dough, which needs to rise for one hour. The result is a fluffy, true pizza crust–like dough that everyone will love. The second version is great if you're in a pinch; it's my 25-minute no-yeast dough and it's fluffy, moist and super soft. Both are delicious—you can't go wrong!

CLASSIC YEAST DOUGH

1 cup (240 ml) warmed almond milk (microwaved for about 45 seconds)

¼ cup (60 ml) melted vegan butter or olive oil

½ tsp salt

1 tbsp (12 g) active dry yeast

2 tsp (9 g) baking powder (only use if baking with gluten-free flour)

1 tbsp (15 ml) cider vinegar (only use if baking with gluten-free flour)

2½ cups (313 g) regular or gluten-free all-purpose flour (for gluten-free, I like Cup4Cup or King Arthur Gluten Free Measure for Measure), plus more for dusting

Nonstick spray, for baking dish

For the Yeast Dough: In a large bowl, mix together the warmed almond milk, melted vegan butter and salt. If you'll be baking with regular flour, evenly sprinkle the yeast over the mixture and stir gently once or twice. If baking with gluten-free flour, add the baking powder and cider vinegar and mix, then sprinkle the top with the yeast. Set aside for 10 minutes.

After 10 minutes, add the flour and mix until a dough forms. With the dough still in the bowl, use your hands to gently form the dough into a mound. Cover the bowl with a clean kitchen towel and let the dough rise for 1 hour. I like to preheat the oven to 350°F (175°C) and set the bowl on top of the warm oven to help it rise more quickly. You will know the dough is done rising when it has nearly doubled in size. If you are using gluten-free flour, the dough will be less voluminous.

Spray a 12-inch (30-cm) baking dish with nonstick spray. Remove the dough from the bowl and place it on a lightly floured surface. Use a rolling pin to roll out the dough to a ⅓-inch (1-cm)-thick rectangular slab. Place the slab of dough in the prepared dish, using your fingers to shape the dough so it fits. Cover the dish with the kitchen towel and allow the dough to rise for another 30 minutes.

If you haven't already done so, preheat the oven to 350°F (175°C). You may place the dish back on top of the preheated oven if you choose. If working with gluten-free flour, you may skip this second rise and proceed to "For the Topping."

(continued)

NO-YEAST DOUGH

1 cup (240 ml) water or unsweetened almond milk

⅓ cup (80 ml) olive oil

1 tsp fresh lemon juice

1 tsp sugar

1½ tsp (7 g) baking powder

2¼ cups (281 g) regular or gluten-free all-purpose flour (for gluten-free, I like King Arthur Gluten Free Measure for Measure), plus more for dusting

Nonstick spray, for baking dish

TOPPING

¼ cup (60 ml) melted vegan butter or olive oil

1 tbsp (9 g) minced garlic

1 tbsp (4 g) chopped fresh parsley

1½ cups (168 g) vegan mozzarella cheese shreds

For the quicker No-Yeast Dough: Preheat the oven to 350°F (175°C). In a large bowl, mix together the water, olive oil, lemon juice, sugar and baking powder. Then, mix in the flour until a thick dough forms.

Spray a 12-inch (30-cm) baking dish with nonstick spray. Remove the dough from the bowl and place it on a lightly floured surface. Use a rolling pin to roll out the dough to a ⅓-inch (1-cm)-thick rectangular slab. Place the slab of dough in the prepared dish, using your fingers to shape the dough so it fits.

For the Topping: In a medium-sized bowl, mix the melted vegan butter with the garlic. Lightly brush the top of the dough with about half of the garlic butter. You should still have plenty left over. Place the dish in the oven and bake for about 25 minutes, or until the top is lightly golden.

While the dough bakes, add the parsley to the remaining garlic butter mixture. Once the bread is done baking, remove it from the oven and sprinkle the vegan mozzarella cheese over the top. Drizzle the herbed garlic butter over the cheese. Return the cheesy bread to the oven and bake for another 5 minutes, or until the cheese is melted.

Cut into 16 strips and serve the cheesy dippers immediately with a side of your favorite store-bought or homemade marinara sauce (page 106).

Incredibly Good Garlic Knots with Homemade Marinara

MAKES 12 knots

ESTIMATED CALORIES:
170 per knot
served with
2 tablespoons
(30 ml) of
marinara

My dad and bonus mom used to take us to the most unbelievable Italian restaurant on weekends. They were known for their garlic knots and always served them in a big basket before the meal. It'll probably come as no surprise that I cared less about the pizza and more about those golden garlic knots drizzled with garlic butter and herbs. None of this sounds vegan to you, does it? This recipe really is vegan, and it really is better than the restaurant version! The smell of the freshly baked dough is irresistible. The texture is identically golden on the outside, fluffy and light on the inside, and the garlic butter on top . . . oh my! Your family just might fight over these and they will never guess that they're vegan!

GARLIC KNOTS

1 cup (240 ml) warmed almond milk (microwaved for about 45 seconds)

¼ cup (60 ml) melted vegan butter or olive oil

½ tsp salt

2 tsp (9 g) baking powder (only use if baking with gluten-free flour)

1 tbsp (15 ml) cider vinegar (only use if baking with gluten-free flour)

1 tbsp (12 g) active dry yeast

2½ cups (313 g) regular or gluten-free all-purpose flour (for gluten-free, I like Cup4Cup or King Arthur Gluten Free Measure for Measure), plus more for dusting

GARLIC BUTTER

¼ cup (60 ml) melted vegan butter or olive oil

2 tsp (6 g) freshly chopped or minced garlic

1 tbsp (5 g) chopped fresh parsley

To prepare the garlic knots: In a large bowl, mix together the warmed almond milk, melted vegan butter and salt. If you'll be using gluten-free flour, add the baking powder and cider vinegar now and mix. Evenly sprinkle the yeast over the mixture and stir gently once or twice. Set aside for 10 minutes.

After 10 minutes, add the flour and mix until a dough forms. With the dough still in the bowl, use your hands to gently form the dough into a mound. Cover the bowl with a clean kitchen towel and let the dough rise for 1 hour. I like to preheat the oven to 350°F (175°C) and set the bowl on top of the warm oven to help it rise more quickly. You will know the dough is done rising when it has nearly doubled in size. If you are using gluten-free flour, the dough will be less voluminous.

If you haven't already done so, preheat the oven to 350°F (175°C). Line a baking sheet with parchment paper.

Remove the dough from the bowl and place it on a floured surface. Use your hands to gently pull the dough apart into 12 equal pieces. Roll each piece into a 5-inch (13-cm)-long strip and then tie each into a loose knot. Place the knots on the prepared baking sheet about 1½ inches (4 cm) apart, leaving room for them to nearly double in size. Once all the knots are on the baking sheet, cover them with a clean kitchen towel and allow them to rise for another 30 minutes. You may set them back on top of the 350°F (175°C) oven if you choose. If using gluten-free flour, you may skip this second rise and proceed to the next step.

Remove the kitchen towel and bake for about 25 minutes, or until they are golden on top and slide easily off the parchment paper.

While the knots bake, prepare the garlic butter topping: In a small bowl, mix together the melted vegan butter, garlic and parsley.

(continued)

QUICK AND EASY HOMEMADE MARINARA SAUCE

2 tbsp (30 ml) olive oil

2 tbsp (17 g) chopped or minced garlic

1 (15-oz [425-g]) canned whole tomatoes

1 (15-oz [425-g]) canned tomato sauce

2 tbsp (10 g) dried oregano

1 tbsp (5 g) dried basil

1 tbsp (5 g) dried parsley

1 tsp garlic powder

½ tsp onion powder

Salt and freshly ground black pepper

¼ cup (20 g) roughly chopped fresh basil (optional)

If making your own marinara sauce, heat the olive oil in a medium-sized saucepan over medium heat. Once the oil is hot, add the garlic and cook for 1 to 2 minutes, or until it sizzles. Add the tomatoes, tomato sauce, oregano, dried basil, dried parsley, garlic powder, onion powder and salt and pepper to taste. Stir and reduce the heat to low once the sauce starts to bubble. Cook over low heat for about 20 minutes. Remove from the heat and stir in the fresh basil (if using). Set aside.

Once the knots are done baking, remove them from the oven, brush with the garlic butter and serve immediately with a side of marinara sauce. These rolls are the perfect pairing for any of your favorite vegan dinners.

Easy Everything but the Bagel Bread

SERVINGS: 12
ESTIMATED CALORIES:
169 per serving

If you're an everything bagel lover, this recipe has your name written all over it. A few years ago, my aunt introduced me to a magical seasoning blend—everything bagel seasoning. Buy it at the store, online or use my quick recipe here to make your own. Serve this loaf at breakfast, brunch or as a savory treat and it'll change your life! Spread it with your favorite vegan butter or vegan cream cheese . . . you'll never look at an everything bagel the same! And your kitchen is going to smell like the unbeatable combination of freshly baked bread and everything bagels! Yum!

EVERYTHING BAGEL SEASONING

1 tbsp (7 g) dried minced garlic

1 tbsp (10 g) dried minced onion

1 tbsp (8 g) white sesame seeds

1 tbsp (8 g) black sesame seeds

1½ tsp (4 g) poppy seeds

1 tsp sea salt flakes

BREAD

1½ cups (360 ml) unsweetened almond milk

¼ cup (60 ml) melted vegan butter

¼ cup (60 ml) olive oil

1 tbsp (15 ml) pure maple syrup

2 tsp (9 g) baking soda

1 tsp baking powder

¼ tsp salt

2¾ cups (344 g) regular or gluten-free all-purpose flour (for gluten-free, I like King Arthur Gluten Free Measure for Measure)

¼ cup (36 g) everything bagel seasoning (my recipe or store-bought)

Preheat the oven to 375°F (190°C). Line a baking sheet with aluminum foil.

Prepare the everything bagel seasoning if not using store-bought: In a small bowl, mix together all the seasoning ingredients.

Make the bread dough: In a large bowl, mix together the almond milk, melted vegan butter, olive oil, maple syrup, baking soda, baking powder and salt. Add the flour and mix until a thick bread dough forms.

Use your hands to form the dough into a mound on the prepared baking sheet. The mound should be 1½ to 2 inches (4 to 5 cm) high. Sprinkle the top with the everything bagel seasoning, loosely cover the loaf with a piece of foil and bake for 45 to 55 minutes.

Remove the bread from the oven, uncover and return to the oven for another 10 minutes. The bread should be golden brown on the outside. Use a toothpick to test the center; it will come out clean when the bread is done. Return the bread to the oven to bake as needed until it's completely cooked in the middle; if the loaf or seasoning begins to brown too much on the outside, cover loosely again with the foil to keep it from burning.

Once the bread is done baking, remove from the oven and allow it to cool for 5 to 10 minutes. Slice and serve with vegan butter or cream cheese.

> TIP: In the mood for a classic slice of thick, crusty bread? Bake this without the everything bagel seasoning. It tastes amazing with a little vegan butter and jam!

Super-Savory Garlic Texas Toast

SERVINGS: 12
ESTIMATED CALORIES:
185 per serving
with topping

Did you grow up loving Texas toast in the freezer aisle of the grocery store? I sure did! My bonus mom always had a box of this shortcut bread in the freezer. This recipe is so much better and just as easy. It has a wonderfully crispy and golden crust that you expect in traditional Texas toast, and when you slice into it, you'll find a soft, fluffy and tender inside—without any eggs or dairy. Don't think this recipe is going to cost you a lot of time in the kitchen; it's a quick bread, which means no yeast and no kneading. Just a golden-crusted homemade garlic bread that everyone will salivate over!

TEXAS LOAF

1½ cups (360 ml) unsweetened almond milk

¼ cup (60 ml) melted vegan butter

¼ cup (60 ml) olive oil

1 tbsp (15 g) granulated or cane sugar

1 tbsp (10 g) minced garlic (optional)

2 tsp (9 g) baking soda

1 tsp baking powder

2¾ cups (344 g) regular or gluten-free all-purpose flour (for gluten-free, I like King Arthur Gluten Free Measure for Measure)

GARLIC & HERB TOPPING

2 tbsp (30 ml) melted vegan butter or olive oil

1 tsp chopped fresh parsley

1 tsp minced garlic

Prepare the Texas loaf: Preheat the oven to 375°F (190°C). Line a baking sheet with aluminum foil.

In a large bowl, mix together the almond milk, melted vegan butter, olive oil, sugar, garlic (if using), baking soda and baking powder. Add the flour and mix until a thick bread dough forms.

Use your hands to form the dough into a mound on the prepared baking sheet. The mound should be 1½ to 2 inches (4 to 5 cm) high. Loosely cover with foil and bake for 45 to 55 minutes, uncovering during the last 10 minutes of baking. The bread should be golden brown on the outside. Use a toothpick to test the center; it will come out clean when the bread is done. Return the bread to the oven to bake until it's completely cooked in the middle. If the loaf begins to brown too much on the outside, cover loosely again with the foil to keep it from burning.

While the bread bakes, prepare the garlic & herb topping: In a small bowl, mix together the melted vegan butter, parsley and garlic.

Once the bread is done baking, remove from the oven and allow it to cool for 5 to 10 minutes. Then, use a brush or spoon to cover the loaf with the topping. Slice and serve this mouthwatering treat immediately.

BAKING FOR BREAKFAST LOVERS

In my first book, I mentioned that many nutrition experts say that breakfast is the most important meal of the day—and I believe it's the most delicious. I saved the best for last, and I'm ending this book with my favorite meal of the day: breakfast! Invite me to enjoy a stack of pancakes drenched in maple syrup, offer me a homemade buttered muffin, serve me a bagel with my coffee or spread a little vegan cream cheese frosting on my cinnamon roll, and I'll basically follow you to the ends of the earth. If you're a breakfast lover like me, this chapter will make your vegan dreams come true!

Each recipe is simple and clocks in under 300 calories per serving (and most under 200). A traditional bagel can be well over 300 calories, but my Any Flavor Bagels (page 114) are right around 100 calories per bagel! Did you have to say farewell to cinnamon rolls when you went vegan or gluten-free? Say hello to your long-lost lover, back and better than ever! My Famous Vegan Cinnamon Rolls (page 121) are a favorite among my family and friends and they all agree—these are some of the best cinnamon rolls they've ever had, and they're so easy! From grab-and-go muffins, donuts, bagels and even Pancake Bread (page 128)—that's right, you heard me—there's something in this chapter that you and everyone in your home will love waking up to. So, pour that coffee, get to baking and in minutes you'll be starting your day on a super-tasty vegan note!

Any Flavor Bagels

SERVINGS: 16

ESTIMATED CALORIES:
112 per plain
bagel

One of my favorite ways to kick off the day is with a hot cup of coffee and a warm bagel. When it comes to bagel flavors, it's hard to choose a favorite. Cinnamon raisin, blueberry, sesame, everything . . . there are too many good options to choose from! Whereas bakery bagels can set you back up to 400 calories, these bagels are a fraction of that. They're easy to make and you can freeze them to grab and pop into your toaster in the morning.

PLAIN BAGELS

1 cup (240 ml) unsweetened almond milk (microwaved for about 45 seconds)

⅓ cup (80 ml) melted vegan butter, divided

2 tbsp (30 ml) pure maple syrup

¼ tsp salt

2 tsp (9 g) baking powder (use only if baking with gluten-free flour)

1 tbsp (15 ml) cider vinegar (use only if baking with gluten-free flour)

1 tbsp (12 g) active dry yeast

2½ cups (313 g) regular or gluten-free all-purpose flour (for gluten-free, I like Cup4Cup or King Arthur Gluten Free Measure for Measure), plus more for dusting

CINNAMON RAISIN (ADDS 9 CALORIES PER BAGEL)

⅓ cup (73 g) raisins

1 tsp ground cinnamon

BLUEBERRY (ADDS 5 CALORIES PER BAGEL)

1 cup (148 g) fresh, frozen or dried blueberries

OTHER TOPPINGS

2 tbsp (36 g) sea salt flakes

2 tbsp (18 g) sesame seeds

2 tbsp (18 g) Everything Seasoning (page 109), or store-bought

2 tbsp (18 g) poppy seeds

Prepare the bagel dough: In a large bowl, use a fork to mix together the warmed almond milk, ¼ cup (60 ml) of the melted vegan butter, maple syrup and salt. If baking with gluten-free flour, add the baking powder and cider vinegar now. Sprinkle the yeast over the mixture and stir two or three times. Allow it to sit for 10 minutes, then add the all-purpose flour and mix until a thick dough forms.

If making cinnamon raisin bagels, use your hands to gently work the raisins and cinnamon into the dough. If making blueberry bagels, carefully work the blueberries into the dough. For other flavors, proceed to the next step. Don't overwork the dough or worry too much about it being evenly combined.

Use your hands to form the dough into a mound, leaving it in the bowl. Cover the bowl with a clean kitchen towel and allow the dough to rise for 1 hour. I like to set my dough on top of a preheated oven to allow it to rise faster. You will know that it has risen when the dough has nearly doubled in size. If using gluten-free flour, the dough will be less voluminous.

Preheat the oven to 350°F (175°C). Line a baking sheet with parchment paper.

Once the dough has risen, roll it into a 1-inch (2.5-cm)-thick slab on a floured surface. Slice the dough into 16 pieces and roll each piece into a 5-inch (13-cm)-long strip. Form each strip into a circular bagel shape and place each bagel on the prepared baking sheet, spacing them about 1½ inches (4 cm) apart. Cover the entire baking sheet with a clean kitchen towel and allow them to rise for 30 minutes. If using gluten-free flour, you may skip the second rise and proceed to the next step.

After the bagels have risen, brush the tops with the remaining melted vegan butter. If desired, top with sea salt, sesame seeds, everything bagel seasoning or poppy seeds. You can also leave them plain. Bake for 15 to 20 minutes, or until the bagels are golden.

Use a knife to slice them in half and enjoy immediately.

Store in an airtight container in the freezer for up to 30 days. Reheat in a toaster or toaster oven and serve plain, or with your favorite vegan butter or cream cheese.

Glazed

Cinnamon Sugar

Powdered Sugar

Choose-Your-Favorite-Flavor Donut Holes

MAKES
60 donut holes

ESTIMATED CALORIES:
34 per plain
donut hole

These baked donut holes are easy like Sunday morning! When my brothers and I were younger, my dad and bonus mom would take us to get donuts after church on Sunday. We loved ordering a big box of donut holes because we could enjoy an assortment of flavors instead of just one. I decided to develop a recipe that was just as cakey, moist, sweet and delicious, but with a bit less sugar, baked and not fried, less greasy, and of course, vegan. The results are more delicious than you can imagine! In under 30 minutes, you'll be enjoying "munchkins" that are perfect with your morning coffee (or for dessert). Choose to enjoy these plain, tossed in confectioners' sugar, cinnamon sugar, or my favorite—glazed. Get ready for a better-than-the-donut-shop experience.

DONUT HOLES

Nonstick spray, for molds

1¼ cups (300 ml) unsweetened almond milk

¼ cup (60 ml) melted vegan butter

1 cup (200 g) cane sugar (see Tip)

1 tsp vanilla extract

1½ tsp (7 g) baking powder

1 tsp baking soda

2 cups (250 g) regular or gluten-free all-purpose flour (for gluten-free, I like King Arthur Gluten Free Measure for Measure)

GLAZE (ADDS 5 CALORIES PER DONUT HOLE)

½ cup (60 g) confectioners' sugar

1 tsp unsweetened almond milk

1 tsp vanilla extract

CINNAMON SUGAR (ADDS 5 CALORIES PER SERVING)

½ tsp ground cinnamon

¼ cup (50 g) cane sugar

POWDERED SUGAR (ADDS 5 CALORIES PER SERVING)

½ cup (60 g) confectioners' sugar

Preheat the oven to 350°F (175°C). Spray 60 silicone donut hole molds or 14 to 16 full-sized donut molds with nonstick spray.

Prepare the donut holes: In a large bowl, use a fork or whisk to mix together the almond milk, melted vegan butter, cane sugar, vanilla, baking powder and baking soda. Then, add the flour and mix until a smooth batter is formed.

Spoon the batter into the prepared molds. Bake for 20 to 25 minutes, or until lightly golden.

While the donuts bake, prepare your topping of choice: If making plain glazed donut holes, in a small bowl, mix together the confectioners' sugar, almond milk and vanilla until smooth.

If making cinnamon sugar donut holes, in a small bowl, mix together the cinnamon and cane sugar. Or, for powdered sugar donut holes, simply pour the confectioners' sugar into a bowl.

Remove the molds from the oven and allow the donut holes to cool, then either brush or drizzle them with the glaze, or toss them in the cinnamon sugar or confectioners' sugar.

Dunk them into coffee, and try to stop yourself from eating the whole batch.

TIP: For even lower-calorie donut holes, use ¼ cup (50 g) of cane sugar plus 4 teaspoons (10 g) of pure powdered stevia in place of a full cup of cane sugar, to make them 28 calories each.

Good Morning Sunshine Oatmeal Muffins

MAKES 16 muffins

ESTIMATED CALORIES: 146 per muffin

Brighten up your morning with these citrusy, deliciously moist and fluffy muffins. Despite being low calorie, they're super flavorful, thanks to the cinnamon and maple syrup. And, they're healthy and filling because of the oats. Plus, they only need about 30 minutes to bake. These wholesome vegan muffins are going to become a morning staple for you and your family. Spread these with a little vegan butter and say: "Good morning, sunshine!"

1 cup (240 ml) unsweetened almond milk

¾ cup (180 ml) pure maple syrup

½ cup (120 ml) fresh orange juice

¼ cup (60 ml) melted vegan butter or coconut oil

1½ tsp (7 g) baking powder

1 tsp baking soda

1 tsp ground cinnamon

2¼ cups (281 g) regular or gluten-free all-purpose flour (for gluten-free, I like King Arthur Gluten Free Measure for Measure)

¾ cup (68 g) quick oats (certified gluten-free, if needed)

Preheat the oven to 375°F (190°C). Line 16 wells of a muffin pan and spray the liners with nonstick cooking spray.

In a large bowl, use a fork or whisk to mix together the almond milk, maple syrup, orange juice, melted vegan butter, baking powder, baking soda and cinnamon until well combined. Add the flour and mix until a loose batter forms. Then, add the quick oats and mix.

Pour the batter into the prepared muffin pan and bake for 25 minutes, or until fluffy and golden.

Serve immediately with a side of fresh orange juice. I love these muffins with a little vegan butter spread on top.

These store well in a resealable plastic bag on the counter for 3 to 5 days.

HEALTHY OAT FLOUR SWAP: Substitute the 2¼ cups (281 g) regular or gluten-free all-purpose flour with 3 cups (375 g) oat flour. This adds 16 calories per muffin.

My Famous Vegan Cinnamon Rolls—2 Ways

MAKES 12 rolls
ESTIMATED CALORIES:
294 per frosted
roll

When I was a kid, my mom would take me to the mall on Saturdays. Shopping was our "thing"! And my thing was Cinnabon. I'd look forward to taking a break between stores to sink my teeth into a buttery, golden and gooey batch of warm cinnamon rolls. Cinnabons aren't vegan-friendly, but I can make a vegan version right at home that's fewer calories and is just as delicious. In fact, I've had friends and family tell me that they prefer my version over any other cinnamon rolls they've tried! Everyone is shocked when they find out that these are vegan.

There are two variations of this recipe, and both will blow your mind. The first is a classic vegan cinnamon roll that uses yeast in the dough. This recipe takes about 2 hours and is well worth the wait. The result is a batch of giant fluffy cinnamon rolls that take your breath away. I've also included a recipe for my easy, no-yeast, 30-minute cinnamon rolls, which are perfect for when you're in a pinch or if you have a yeast allergy. No matter which version you choose, you won't believe how golden, buttery and ooey-gooey-good these are! Drizzle them with vegan cream cheese frosting and you and your family will be licking your plates clean and fighting over the last bite.

CLASSIC YEAST DOUGH

1 cup (240 ml) warmed almond milk (microwaved for about 30 seconds)

¼ cup (60 ml) freshly melted vegan butter

2 tbsp (30 ml) pure maple syrup

½ tsp salt

2 tsp (9 g) baking powder (only use if baking with gluten-free flour)

1 tbsp (15 ml) cider vinegar (only use if baking with gluten-free flour)

1 tbsp (13 g) active dry yeast

2½ cups (312 g) regular or gluten-free all-purpose flour (for gluten-free, I like Cup4Cup or King Arthur Gluten Free Measure for Measure), plus more for dusting

Nonstick spray, for dish

Prepare the dough: In a large bowl, use a fork to mix together the warmed almond milk, freshly melted vegan butter, maple syrup and salt. If baking with gluten-free flour, mix in the baking powder and cider vinegar. Next, sprinkle the yeast evenly over the top of the mixture and allow it to sit for about 10 minutes. Then, stir in the flour until a dough forms.

Use your hands to gently form the dough into a round mound. Be careful not to overwork the dough. Leave the dough in the bowl and cover it with a clean kitchen towel. Allow it to rise for 1 hour. I like to set the dough on top of a preheated oven to help it rise faster. You will know it has risen when it has nearly doubled in size. If you are using gluten-free flour, the dough will be less voluminous.

Spray a 10- to 12-inch (25- to 30-cm) casserole dish with nonstick spray. Once the dough has risen, lay it on a well-floured surface and roll it out to a ⅓-inch (1-cm)-thick rectangle. Sprinkle more flour on top if the dough is too sticky to roll.

(continued)

FILLING

¼ cup (57 g) softened vegan butter

½ cup (100 g) cane sugar

2 tbsp (24 g) ground cinnamon

VEGAN CREAM CHEESE FROSTING

2 oz (57 g) vegan cream cheese

2 tbsp (28 g) softened vegan butter

¾ cup (90 g) confectioners' sugar

Add the filling: Spread the softened vegan butter evenly onto the dough and then sprinkle the sugar and cinnamon over the top. Carefully roll up your dough into a log and slice it into about 12 equal-width pinwheels. If you are using gluten-free flour, the dough will be more fragile so take your time. If it falls apart while rolling, simply use your hands to form it back together.

Place the pinwheels into your prepared casserole dish, making sure that there is enough room for them to double in size. Cover the dish loosely with the kitchen towel and set aside for 30 minutes to allow them to rise. Set them on top of the preheated oven again if you choose. You will know they are done rising when they have nearly doubled in size. If you are using gluten-free flour, you may skip the second rise and proceed to baking.

Preheat the oven to 350°F (175°C). Remove the kitchen towel from the rolls and bake them for 30 to 35 minutes, or until golden.

While the rolls bake, prepare the frosting: In a medium-sized bowl, use an electric hand mixer to mix together the vegan cream cheese, softened vegan butter and confectioners' sugar.

Once the rolls are done baking, remove them from the oven and wait 5 to 10 minutes for them to cool before spreading the frosting over the top. Serve warm and try not to eat the entire dish!

Quick 30-Minute No-Yeast Cinnamon Rolls

MAKES 12 ROLLS
ESTIMATED CALORIES:
284 per frosted roll

NO-YEAST DOUGH

¾ cup (180 ml) unsweetened almond milk

½ cup (120 ml) melted vegan butter

1½ tsp (7 g) baking powder

2 cups (250 g) regular or gluten-free all-purpose flour (for gluten-free, I like Cup4Cup or King Arthur Gluten Free Measure for Measure), plus more for dusting

Nonstick spray, for dish

FILLING

¼ cup (57 g) softened vegan butter

⅓ cup (67 g) cane sugar

2 tbsp (24 g) ground cinnamon

VEGAN CREAM CHEESE FROSTING

2 oz (57 g) vegan cream cheese

2 tbsp (28 g) softened vegan butter

¾ cup (90 g) confectioners' sugar

Preheat the oven to 400°F (200°C). In a large bowl, use a fork to mix together the almond milk, melted vegan butter and baking powder. Then, mix in the flour until a thick dough forms.

Spray an 8- to 10-inch (20- to 25-cm) casserole dish with nonstick spray. Lay the dough on a floured surface and roll it out a ¼-inch (6-mm)-thick rectangle. You may need to sprinkle a little flour on top if the dough is too sticky to roll. Add the filling: Spread the softened vegan butter onto the rolled dough, then sprinkle the cane sugar and cinnamon over the top. Roll up the dough into a log and slice it into about 12 equal-width pinwheels.

Place the pinwheels into the prepared casserole dish. Set the rolls close enough together to where they are almost touching each other.

Bake them for 20 minutes, or until lightly golden. If desired, broil them for 1 to 2 minutes at the end to give them more color.

While the rolls bake, prepare the frosting: In a medium-sized bowl, use an electric mixer to mix together the vegan cream cheese, softened vegan butter and confectioners' sugar.

Once the rolls are done baking, remove them from the oven and wait 5 to 10 minutes for them to cool before spreading the frosting over the top, then dive right in.

Brown Sugar–Cinnamon Swirl Banana Bread

SERVINGS: 12
ESTIMATED CALORIES:
188 per serving

Among my family and friends, I am known for my banana breads—it's my go-to baked good to bring to any gathering. I'm always trying new variations, such as adding fruit, chocolate and, in this case, brown sugar and cinnamon. Yum! I've never met a slice of banana bread I didn't like. But there are just some versions that stand out from the crowd. This bread is a showstopper and a crowd-pleaser! I've said this before—vegan banana bread is so much better than non-vegan! Each dense slice is soft, tender and buttery and the rich flavor combination is out of this world. Give this a try at your next festive occasion and everyone will be begging you for the recipe. Oh, and your kitchen is going to smell incredible!

BANANA BREAD

Nonstick spray, for pan

3 overripe bananas, mashed

1¼ cups (300 ml) unsweetened almond milk

¼ cup (60 ml) melted vegan butter

½ cup (100 g) cane, coconut or light brown sugar

1 tsp vanilla extract

2 tsp (9 g) baking powder

1 tsp baking soda

2 cups (250 g) regular or gluten-free all-purpose flour (for gluten-free, I like King Arthur Gluten Free Measure for Measure)

1 tbsp (8 g) ground cinnamon

TOPPING

3 tbsp (42 g) light brown sugar

1 tbsp (15 ml) melted vegan butter

Preheat the oven to 375°F (190°C). Spray a 9 x 5–inch (23 x 13–cm) loaf pan with nonstick spray.

In a large bowl, use a fork to mix together the bananas, almond milk, melted vegan butter, cane sugar, vanilla, baking powder and baking soda. Add the flour and mix until a batter forms.

Spoon half of the batter evenly into the prepared loaf pan. Sprinkle the cinnamon over the top of the batter and use a fork or knife to swirl it a couple of times. Then, pour the remaining batter evenly over the top.

Add the topping: Sprinkle the top of the batter with the brown sugar, then drizzle with the melted vegan butter.

Bake for 50 to 60 minutes, or until you can stick a toothpick in the center of the loaf and it comes out clean.

Remove the banana bread from the pan and allow it to cool for about 5 minutes. Slice and serve warm.

7-Ingredient Sheet Pan Banana Pancakes

MAKES
16 pancakes
ESTIMATED CALORIES:
69 per pancake

Y'all, these are the best banana pancakes and they are so easy (and versatile). Fluffy, golden, light as air and drizzled with maple syrup, this is the perfect stack of pancakes and a recipe that's so simple and delicious that it will wind up on your family's weekly menu. Anyone can make these and no one will believe this recipe is vegan, gluten-free optional and low calorie. This recipe uses just seven simple ingredients and one bowl. The best part is that it will only take you 5 minutes to mix and you can continue on with your morning routine! Twenty minutes later, you'll have a tasty golden stack of fluffy banana pancakes that everyone is going to absolutely love! If desired, mix your favorite berries or even chocolate chips into the batter to change it up.

Nonstick spray, for pan

2 large overripe bananas, mashed

2 cups (480 ml) unsweetened almond milk

¼ cup (60 ml) pure maple syrup

4 tsp (18 g) baking powder

2 tsp (10 ml) vanilla extract

1 tsp ground cinnamon

2 cups (250 g) regular or gluten-free all-purpose flour (for gluten-free, I like King Arthur Gluten Free Measure for Measure)

Berries or vegan chocolate chips (optional; calories vary)

Preheat the oven to 350°F (175°C). Spray a rimmed baking sheet with nonstick spray.

In a large bowl, use a fork or whisk to mix together the bananas, almond milk, maple syrup, baking powder, vanilla and cinnamon. Add the flour and mix until the batter is smooth. If using, fold in the berries or chocolate chips.

Transfer the batter to the prepared baking sheet. Bake for about 20 minutes, or until the pancakes are golden around the edges.

Slice the pancakes into about 16 squares and serve plated with fresh berries and maple syrup. I've also enjoyed these with nut butter or sprinkled with nuts!

Mouthwatering Maple Syrup Pancake Bread

SERVING: 14
ESTIMATED CALORIES:
171 per serving

Fill your kitchen will the smell of homemade bread and the taste of flapjacks with this scrumptious recipe. This homemade vegan bread tastes like a stack of warm fluffy pancakes. I was inspired to create this recipe because I was a picky eater as a kid. But there were a few foods I never turned down: bread and pancakes (oh, and cookies). This recipe is vegan, can be made gluten-free and uses oats, making each slice healthy, filling and delicious. No bread maker needed—just one bowl and a few simple ingredients! The result is a golden loaf of soft, fluffy bread that will remind you of your favorite breakfast stack. If you have any picky eaters in your home, this is a must-try. Drizzle it with maple syrup and know that you've been warned . . . it's addictive!

Nonstick spray, for pan

1 cup (240 ml) unsweetened almond milk

1 cup (240 ml) pure maple syrup

¼ cup (60 ml) melted vegan butter

1 tsp vanilla extract

1½ tsp (7 g) baking powder

1 tsp baking soda

½ tsp ground cinnamon

2 cups (250 g) regular or gluten-free all-purpose flour (for gluten-free, I like King Arthur Gluten Free Measure for Measure)

1 cup (90 g) quick oats (certified gluten-free, if needed)

Preheat the oven to 375°F (190°C). Spray a 9 x 5–inch (23 x 13–cm) loaf pan with nonstick spray.

In a medium-sized bowl, use a fork or whisk to mix together the almond milk, maple syrup, melted vegan butter, vanilla, baking powder, baking soda and cinnamon. Add the flour and mix until a smooth batter is formed. Then, stir in the quick oats.

Pour the batter into the prepared loaf pan and bake for about 40 minutes, or until the loaf is completely risen and golden brown on top. Test the center with a toothpick; when it comes out clean, the bread is done.

Remove the loaf from the pan and serve sliced and drizzled with maple syrup or spread with a little vegan butter. Serve with fresh berries and your favorite breakfast sides.

This bread stores well in an airtight container on the counter for up to 3 days.

Grab-and-Go Mixed Berry Muffins

No one will be able to resist grabbing one of these mixed berry muffins on the way out the door! Muffins were a common grab-and-go breakfast in my family's home while I was growing up. My mom and I would bake a batch early in the week and heat them up in the microwave each morning—always spread with a little butter! That being said, we usually used packaged mixes—but this recipe is so easy, you won't need to! It takes about 5 minutes to prep and 20 minutes to bake. No eggs or dairy necessary. In less than 30 minutes, you'll have a warm and fresh batch of homemade muffins that are fluffy, moist and oh so scrumptious. Friends and family who have tried this recipe have told me they are the best muffins they've ever made. So, go ahead and grab one . . . they're so low-cal that you can grab a few!

MAKES
14 to 16 muffins

ESTIMATED CALORIES:
106 per muffin

Nonstick spray, for muffin liners

1 ripe banana, mashed

1 cup (240 ml) unsweetened almond milk

¼ cup (60 ml) pure maple syrup

⅓ cup (80 ml) melted vegan butter

4 tsp (10 g) pure powdered stevia (see Tip)

½ tsp baking soda

2 tsp (9 g) baking powder

1½ cups (188 g) regular or gluten-free all-purpose flour (for gluten-free, I like King Arthur Gluten Free Measure for Measure)

½ cup (74 g) fresh or frozen wild blueberries

½ cup (84 g) diced fresh or frozen strawberries

Preheat the oven to 375°F (190°C). Line 14 to 16 wells of a muffin pan. I like to spray the liners with nonstick spray to make sure they don't stick.

In a large bowl, using a fork, mix together the mashed banana, almond milk, maple syrup, melted vegan butter, stevia, baking soda and baking powder. Mix in the flour until the batter is smooth. Fold in the blueberries and strawberries.

Pour the batter into the prepared muffin pan. Bake for 25 to 30 minutes, or until the muffins have completely risen and are golden on the top.

Remove the muffins from the pan and serve them warm with a little softened vegan butter.

Store in an airtight container at room temperature for up to 3 days.

TIP: No stevia? No problem! Use ¾ cup (150 g) of cane sugar in place of the stevia. This swap will add only 37 calories to each muffin.

HEALTHY OAT FLOUR SWAP: Substitute the 1½ cups (188 g) regular or gluten-free all-purpose flour with 2 cups (250 g) oat flour. This adds 14 calories per muffin.

Chocolate Powdered Sugar Donuts

MAKES 16 donuts
ESTIMATED CALORIES: 140 per donut

Am I the only one who grew up loving those packaged powdered sugar donuts you could find in almost any snack food aisle or vending machine? I decided to go on a mission to make a better-for-you and better-tasting version. Improving this recipe was easy because anything homemade is going to taste better. These donuts are also vegan and less greasy because they're baked and not fried. If you've never had a chocolate powdered sugar donut, these will change your life. These are so easy and they are the perfect chocolaty treat to sink your teeth into. Serve them for dessert, breakfast or just a sweet tasty snack. Oh, and did I mention . . . only 140 calories each? These donuts are a chocolate lover's childhood dream come true!

Nonstick spray, for molds

1⅓ cups (320 ml) unsweetened almond milk

¼ cup (60 ml) melted vegan butter

1 cup (200 g) cane or coconut sugar (see Tip)

1 tsp baking soda

1½ tsp (7 g) baking powder

1 tsp vanilla extract

¼ cup (22 g) unsweetened cocoa powder

2 cups (250 g) regular or gluten-free all-purpose flour (for gluten-free, I like King Arthur Gluten Free Measure for Measure)

¼ cup (32 g) confectioners' sugar

Preheat the oven to 350°F (175°C). Spray 16 silicone donut molds with nonstick spray. No donut molds? No problem! You can make these into muffins by lining 16 muffin wells. I like to lightly spray my paper liners with nonstick spray.

In a large bowl, use a fork or whisk to mix together the almond milk, melted vegan butter, cane sugar, baking soda, baking powder and vanilla. Then, add the cocoa powder and whisk until smooth. Add the flour to the chocolate mixture and mix until just combined. The batter will be thick; don't overmix, or else the donuts will become dense.

Pour the batter into the prepared donut molds. Bake for 20 to 25 minutes, or until the donuts have completely risen.

Once the donuts are done baking, remove them from the molds and allow them to cool for 2 to 3 minutes. Then, toss them in the confectioners' sugar and sink your teeth in.

> **TIP:** In the mood for an even lower-calorie donut? Swap out the full cup (200 g) of the cane or coconut sugar for ¼ cup (50 g) of sugar plus 4 teaspoons (10 g) of pure powdered stevia to make 104-calorie donuts.

Peanut Butter and Jelly Oatmeal Breakfast Bars

MAKES 12 bars
ESTIMATED CALORIES: 160 per bar

As most of you know, Peanut Butter and Jilly is the name of my vegan and gluten-free recipe blog. And, if you haven't picked up on it by now, peanut butter and jelly is one of my favorite nostalgic treats. Whether baking it into a baked oatmeal, a sweet roll, or just going with the good old-fashioned PB&J sandwich, the combo never fails. Prepare to get hooked on these peanut butter and jelly bars. Not only will they remind you of your childhood, but they're filling, made with healthy oats and slathered with creamy peanut butter and jelly. Make these for a tasty wholesome grab-and-go breakfast or snack. This is a family-favorite treat that kids (and adults) will love!

Nonstick spray, for dish

½ cup (120 ml) unsweetened almond milk

2 tbsp (30 ml) melted vegan butter

2 tbsp (30 ml) pure maple syrup

1 tsp baking powder

1 tsp vanilla extract

¼ tsp ground cinnamon

2 cups (180 g) quick oats (certified gluten-free, if needed)

½ cup (120 ml) melted peanut butter (melt in a microwave)

½ cup (120 ml) of your favorite jam or jelly (calories vary; I used Trader Joe's Reduced Sugar Organic Strawberry Preserves)

Preheat the oven to 350°F (175°C). Spray a 9 x 11–inch (23 x 28–cm) casserole dish with nonstick spray.

In a large bowl, use a fork to mix together the almond milk, melted vegan butter, maple syrup, baking powder, vanilla and cinnamon. Mix in the quick oats until the mixture is completely combined.

Pour the mixture into the prepared casserole dish. Cover the dish with aluminum foil and bake for 20 minutes. Remove from the oven—the oats should be completely cooked in the center. Remove the foil and return to the oven for an additional 5 to 10 minutes, or until lightly golden around the edges.

Remove from the oven, let cool, then chill in the fridge for 30 minutes before slicing and serving. Once the bars have chilled and you are about to serve them, in a microwave-safe dish, warm your peanut butter and jam separately in a microwave for 20 to 30 seconds. Slice the oatmeal slab into 12 bars and drizzle them with the melted peanut butter and jam.

Bakery-Style Chocolate Chip Oat Muffins

MAKES 16 muffins
ESTIMATED CALORIES: 149 per muffin

There is no better way to wake up than with a batch of freshly baked muffins. Skip the bakery and whip up this recipe in the comfort of your home! You need just nine simple ingredients and about 5 minutes to prepare them. No eggs or dairy are needed, making them a lighter and healthier version of this beloved treat. These are perfect to make ahead on busy weekday mornings and will save you time and calories!

1¼ cups (300 ml) almond milk

¼ cup (60 ml) melted vegan butter

1 cup (200 g) coconut or cane sugar (see Tip)

1½ tsp (7 g) baking powder

1 tsp baking soda

1 tsp vanilla extract

1½ cups (187 g) regular or gluten-free all-purpose flour (for gluten-free, I like King Arthur Gluten Free Measure for Measure)

1 cup (90 g) quick oats (certified gluten-free, if needed)

¼ cup (42 g) vegan chocolate chips

Preheat the oven to 350°F (175°C). Line 16 wells of a muffin pan and spray the liners with nonstick cooking spray.

In a large bowl, use a fork or whisk to mix together the almond milk, melted vegan butter, sugar, baking powder, baking soda and vanilla. Mix in the flour and oats just until the batter is smooth. Fold in the vegan chocolate chips.

Pour the batter into the lined muffin wells. Bake for 25 minutes, or until they have completely risen and a toothpick inserted into the center of one comes out clean.

These store well for up to 3 days in an airtight container at room temperature.

TIP: Looking for a low-calorie sugar substitute? Swap out the 1 cup (200 g) of sugar for ¼ cup (50 g) of sugar plus 4 teaspoons (10 g) of pure powdered stevia. This will give you muffins that are 134 calories each. Alternatively, you may use as little as ½ cup (100 g) of sugar in this recipe, reducing the calories by about 8.

Make-Ahead Blueberry Mini Muffins

MAKES
60 mini muffins / 16 standard muffins

ESTIMATED CALORIES:
31 per mini muffin / 118 per standard muffin

You can't go wrong with a blueberry muffin. Have you ever had one of those blueberry muffin snack packs? If so, these are better-tasting and a better-for-your-waistline version! You'd never know they're vegan because of how fluffy, moist and soft they are. Plus, they're made with less sugar than most blueberry muffins, yet hit the spot just the same. These are a favorite among my family and friends. Make them in a big batch and grab them when you have a hankering for a tasty treat. You can also make full-sized muffins for a yummy homemade vegan breakfast!

Coconut oil or olive oil spray, if using paper liners

1¼ cups (300 ml) unsweetened almond milk

¼ cup (60 ml) melted vegan butter

¾ cup (150 g) cane sugar (see Tip)

1 tsp vanilla extract

1½ tsp (7 g) baking powder

1 tsp baking soda

2 cups (250 g) regular or gluten-free all-purpose flour (for gluten-free, I like King Arthur Gluten Free Measure for Measure)

1 cup (148 g) fresh or frozen wild blueberries

Preheat the oven to 375°F (190°C). Line 60 silicone mini muffin molds or 16 standard muffin wells with paper liners. I like to spray them lightly with a little coconut oil or olive oil spray to keep them from sticking to the paper.

In a large bowl, use a fork or whisk to mix together the almond milk, melted vegan butter, sugar, vanilla, baking powder and baking soda. Then, add the flour and mix until a silky batter is formed. Fold in the blueberries.

Spoon the batter into the prepared muffin molds or pan.

Bake for 20 to 25 minutes, or until the muffins are golden brown. Remove from the molds or pan and serve warm. They taste amazing on their own or spread with nut butter or vegan butter.

Store the muffins in an airtight container on the counter for 2 to 3 days, or freeze for up to 30 days.

TIP: To reduce the sugar in this recipe, you may use ¼ cup (50 g) of cane sugar plus 1 or 2 teaspoons (3 to 5 g) of pure powdered stevia in place of the ¾ cup (150 g) cane sugar. This swap results in 25 calorie mini muffins or 94 calorie full-sized muffins.

Easy Cinnamon Sugar Bagel Bites

Bagel bites are as fun and easy to bake as they are to eat! Traditional bagels can be high in calories and not very nutritious. Thanks to the filling flaxseed meal, these bites are a little better for ya! Toss them in coconut sugar (or cane sugar) and they become even more wholesome. These bagel bites are perfect served solo with coffee. Take them to the next level by enjoying them with vegan butter or cream cheese.

MAKES 18 bites
ESTIMATED CALORIES: 53 per bite

2 tbsp (20 g) flaxseed meal

6 tbsp (90 ml) warm water

½ cup (120 ml) unsweetened almond milk

2 tbsp (30 ml) olive oil

2 tsp (9 g) baking powder

½ tsp salt

1 cup (125 g) regular or gluten-free all-purpose flour (for gluten-free, I like King Arthur Gluten Free Measure for Measure)

¼ cup (50 g) coconut or cane sugar

1 tsp ground cinnamon

Coconut oil or olive oil spray (optional)

Preheat the oven to 400°F (200°C). Have ready 18 silicone donut hole, cake pop or mini muffin molds.

In a small bowl, mix the flaxseed meal with the warm water. Set aside for 2 minutes, or until a gel forms, to make flax eggs.

In a medium-sized bowl, mix together the almond milk, olive oil, baking powder and salt. Then, add the flax eggs while they're still warm and mix to incorporate. Add the flour and mix until a thick dough forms.

Scoop the bagel dough into your choice of molds. Bake for 10 to 12 minutes, or until the bites have risen and are lightly golden.

While the bagel bites bake, in a small bowl, mix together the sugar and cinnamon. After baking, while the bagel bites are still warm, toss them in the cinnamon sugar mixture. If the cinnamon sugar doesn't stick, spray the bites first with a little coconut oil or olive oil spray and toss in the cinnamon sugar.

Serve these delectable bites immediately spread with a little vegan butter or cream cheese. If desired, toast them before serving to give them that crisp bagel texture.

Glazed Strawberry Donuts

MAKES 14 to 16 donuts

ESTIMATED CALORIES: 149 per glazed donut

My family always picked up donuts on Sunday mornings after church. We'd get a big box with various flavors, but my brothers and I would always fight over who got to hold the box on the car ride home—I think it was because we wanted the first choice. And these are mine!

These cakey strawberry donuts will make you never need to step foot out of the house again to indulge in that donut shop treat we all love! They're baked, not fried, to tender perfection—glazed on the outside and super-moist on the inside. Donut shop fried donuts usually set you back up to 400 calories; these strawberry donuts are a fraction of that. They're super easy, vegan and can be whipped up in less time than it would take you to drive over to the donut shop! My favorite part of this recipe is how versatile they are. You can use any berries in place of the strawberries and the results will always be too good for words!

. . . .

STRAWBERRY DONUTS

Nonstick spray, for molds

1¼ cups (300 ml) unsweetened almond milk

1 cup (200 g) cane sugar (see Tip)

¼ cup (60 ml) melted vegan butter

1 tsp baking soda

1½ tsp (7 g) baking powder

1 tsp vanilla extract

2 cups (250 g) regular or gluten-free all-purpose flour (for gluten-free, I like King Arthur Gluten Free Measure for Measure)

1 cup (150 g) diced fresh or frozen strawberries

VANILLA GLAZE

½ cup (60 g) confectioners' sugar

1 tbsp (15 ml) unsweetened almond milk

1 tsp vanilla extract

Prepare the donuts: Preheat the oven to 350°F (175°C). Spray 14 to 16 silicone donut molds with nonstick spray.

In a large bowl, use a fork to mix together the almond milk, cane sugar, melted vegan butter, baking soda, baking powder and vanilla. Then, mix in the flour until just combined.

Gently fold the strawberries into the batter and pour the batter into the prepared donut molds. Bake for about 20 minutes, or until the donuts are golden.

They're perfectly sweet on their own, or prepare the glaze: In a small bowl, use a whisk to mix together the confectioners' sugar, almond milk and vanilla.

Remove the donuts from the molds and allow them to cool for about 2 minutes before spooning the glaze over the top.

TIP: Craving an even lower-calorie strawberry donut? Use ¼ cup (50 g) of cane sugar plus 4 tsp (10 g) of pure powdered stevia. You'll enjoy a 110-calorie glazed (95 unglazed) donut without sacrificing any of the cakey, sweet and delicious flavors you love.

Sunshine Maple-Buttered Biscuits

MAKES 16 biscuits
ESTIMATED CALORIES:
140 per biscuit

Welcome to vegan paradise, we have biscuits! When my brother and I were growing up, my mom used to bake canned biscuits for breakfast or dessert. She would drizzle them with the most delicious mixture of honey and butter. These homemade vegan biscuits are inspired by her. If you loved those prepackaged biscuits as I did growing up, then these are going to hit the spot! They're made in minutes, use simple ingredients, are lightly sweet, perfectly buttery and oh my, they are good! Serve them for an indulgent vegan breakfast or brunch, or use them as buns for a breakfast sandwich.

BISCUITS

½ cup (120 ml) unsweetened almond milk

½ cup (120 ml) melted vegan butter

¼ cup (60 ml) fresh orange juice

¼ cup (60 ml) pure maple syrup

2 tsp (9 g) baking powder

2 tsp (10 ml) vanilla extract

2¼ cups (281 g) regular or gluten-free all-purpose flour (for gluten-free, I like King Arthur Gluten Free Measure for Measure), plus more for dusting

MAPLE BUTTER

2 tbsp (30 ml) pure maple syrup

2 tbsp (30 ml) melted vegan butter

Prepare the biscuits: Preheat the oven to 400°F (200°C). Line a baking sheet with parchment paper.

In a large bowl, use a fork to mix together the almond milk, melted vegan butter, orange juice, maple syrup, baking powder and vanilla. Then, add the flour and mix just until a dough forms. Be careful not to overwork the dough, or else it will become dense.

On a floured surface, use a rolling pin to roll out the dough into a rectangle about ⅓ inch (1 cm) thick, fold it in half and use your rolling pin to roll it back out to a ⅓-inch (1-cm)-thick rectangle. Repeat this two more times, ending with a ⅓-inch (1-cm)-thick rectangular slab of dough.

Use a knife to slice the dough into 16 squares. Place them about 1½ inches (4 cm) apart on the prepared baking sheet. Bake for 15 minutes, or until the biscuits are golden and have all risen. If desired, broil at the end for 1 minute to give them more color.

While the biscuits bake, prepare the maple butter: In a small bowl, mix together the maple syrup and melted vegan butter.

Remove the biscuits from the oven as soon as they're done. Once they've cooled for a few minutes, brush or drizzle the maple butter over the top of the biscuits, or serve the glaze on the side as a dipping sauce.

ACKNOWLEDGMENTS

So much love is baked into this cookbook. To God, for without you, none of this would be possible.

To the incredible team at Page Street Publishing, a heartfelt thank-you for believing in me and making my vegan dreams a reality. I don't know what I'd do without my incredible editor, Caitlin. I am so thankful to Lauren, senior editor, for overseeing my work throughout the development of this baking book. A special thanks to Meg P. from business and production for everything you do! Meg B. and Laura, thank you for creating another beautifully delicious design to showcase my recipes and photos. Mina and Charlotte, for answering all of my questions and taking such care in marketing this book.

To my friends who have become a part of my family: I thank God for bringing each and every one of you into my life. Over the years, we have all gone through so much. Things have changed as "life has happened," but one thing that has never changed is how we are here for each other through thick and thin. A special thank you to Dr. Jyll Walsh for rearranging her busy schedule on multiple occasions to help me with the creation of this book.

Now, here come the real waterworks: Mama, so many of the recipes in this book are inspired by our mother-daughter moments together. You are my best friend, my greatest role model, my strength and the origin of my sweet tooth. Dad, the biggest fan of my pumpkin pie. Thank you for always inspiring me to dream big and to never stop listening to my heart. You've taught me how to put others first, and to never stop trying to spread love in this world. To my not so little brothers: Jameson, Sam G. and Sam B. ("Sweet Potato"). You're all grown up now, but I will never stop seeing you as my little brothers who I had to share my donuts with. To my bonus parents: our family has been blended and unblended too many times to count. But you all have taught me that family is not about blood, but love. Mo, Laura, Ronnie, thank you for the love and friendships we will forever share. To my friends and relatives, you were the best recipe tasters a girl could ask for, and your encouragement was so greatly appreciated.

To my readers, I cannot thank you enough for trusting me to create yummy vegan and gluten-free recipes for you and the ones you love. Thank you for your support, your kindness, for trying my recipes and giving your invaluable feedback. This book is for you. I hope each vegan treat brings a smile to your face and fills your home and tummy with oven-baked happiness.

ABOUT THE AUTHOR

JILLIAN GLENN, author of *Easy Low-Cal Vegan Eats*, is a popular vegan and gluten-free recipe creator and a trusted source for easy, low-calorie vegan and gluten-free recipes. Her blog, Peanut Butter and Jilly, has become a favored guide for slimmed-down vegan eats and has received national press from NBC, CBS, ABC's *Good Morning America* and more. All of her recipes are plant-based, can be made gluten-free and are absolutely mouthwatering. She uses affordable, easy-to-find ingredients and simple instructions to create her crave-worthy comfort foods. She has a certification in nutrition, prioritizes health and wellness and also has a major sweet tooth. She believes living a healthy lifestyle includes indulgences and never denies herself the foods she loves! To learn more and connect with Jillian, check out her blog at PeanutButterandJilly.com.

INDEX